FIRST IMPRESSIONS, LASTING IMPRESSIONS

Projecting a powerful image in the first few seconds can change your entire life

RAKESH AGARWAL & SUMAN AGARWAL

FIRST IMPRESSIONS, LASTING IMPRESSIONS

First Published in 2013

Published by
Bennett, Coleman & Co. Ltd.,
7, Bahadur Shah Zafar Marg,
New Delhi - 110002

Edited, Designed, Marketed & Distributed by

Times Group Books

Times Group Books
(A division of Bennett, Coleman and Company Limited)
Times Annexe, 9-10, Bahadur Shah Zafar Marg, New Delhi-110002

Printed at: Nutech Photolithographers

ISBN 978-93-80942-91-9

Price: ₹249

Contents

Foreword

Do you want to achieve your dreams? Then get some training in the way you present yourself. A developing country like India has very few institutes which impart training in communications, etiquette, body language, wardrobing, or grooming. Even basic training in these areas would literally transform people in terms of their appearance, their demeanour, and their lives. While India's growing middle class has had the benefit of some training in self-presentation they still need more as they advance into business roles, enabling them to take their place in a global economy. Together, Rakesh and Suman intend to fill this gap for image education for all.

Forward thinkers that they are, Rakesh and Suman have created an educational arena primed to benefit both individuals and India as a whole. Targeting the masses, their business model is meticulously planned out, structured to attract intelligent and entrepreneurial individuals to receive a comprehensive education in image management. They, in turn, will take segmented units of image information to individuals in the form of private consultations, to corporate and business groups in seminars and workshops, as well as to community groups in short courses.

In this book, they ask the reader to consider their many questions to get us thinking and talking about appearance, self-presentation, and the image we reflect or project. They aim to prepare us to recognize the first impressions that we create within the various spheres of our lives and the influence those impressions have on the relationships we form and on the achievement of our personal and professional goals.

Most of us are anxious to improve our lives, but we are often unwilling or unsure of how to improve ourselves and therefore never move forward. The need to improve our self-presentation, our perceptions of ourselves and the impressions we create on others is essential to our personal and professional success in life. The work we do on ourselves is much more significant when we recognize its effect on others, as well as ourselves — who we are and who we could become. It's never too late to become the person we want to be.

Read this book carefully and ponder on its significance, believing in your potential. When we are able to present ourselves appropriately, authentically, attractively, and affordably, we are better able to create powerful positive first and lasting impressions-enabling us to forget ourselves and enjoy the freedom of moving forward toward the achievement of our personal and professional goals.

Judith Rasband MS, AICI CIM
CEO Conselle LC
Executive Director — Conselle Institute of Image Management

Acknowledgements

We would never have been able to bring out this book without the support of several people and we are indebted to them.

We thank Judith Rasband, the Image Guru and our curriculum partner. Our interactions with her generated the idea of writing this book. She has been an invaluable support during the entire process of starting and putting together what is a very complex topic in a simple manner.

We thank Madhuri Y and Web of Comms. Without their research and constant support in writing, correcting and re-writing this book, it would never have happened.

Madhuri Y, an alumnus of the Indian Institute of Management-Ahmedabad, is the writer of children's fiction and adult non-fiction. Web of Comms, founded by IIM-A alumnus Lira Priyadarsani, is a full service marketing agency, offering strategic and customer-centric services across all media.

Rakesh Agarwal &
Suman Agarwal

Chapter 1

What are First Impressions?

First impressions are a constant in society... Good ones are pleasant and long lasting, bad ones long and difficult to disprove.

— Diego Velasquez
Spanish Painter and Leading Artist in the Court of King Philip IV

It was a warm Friday afternoon in Mumbai and Nilima had walked into our office. A friend for years, she had just attended an interview. Judging by her demeanour, Suman and I knew it had not gone well.

"I was in for not more than 15 minutes and the interview was over," said Nilima. "Tell me Rakesh, is that all it takes to judge me?"

"A lot less than that," I corrected her. "A few seconds is all they would have taken to come to a conclusion."

"How's that possible?" she asked, raising her hands in defeat.

"First impressions," I said. "They would have formed a first impression of you within the first few seconds. And then yes, they would have continued the interview, asking you questions to judge your skills, competence and all the things they need to tick off on their list. But, sorry to say, it was the first few seconds that had the greatest impact."

Nilima was incredulous. "A few seconds? That can't be true. It's barely enough time to walk in and give a round of handshakes. I might have said a 'hello' at the most. What about my capability, the details of my experience, how I performed, what I achieved..? There's so much more to it."

I shook my head. "Let me give you an example. How do you judge music...new music?"

"I listen for a few seconds," she said and paused. Then she continued slowly, "In those few seconds I know... I just know... whether I like it or not. Then I flip to the next track or continue listening."

"So, before you go into your next interview, ask yourself whether you have prepared for those first few seconds."

So, what are first impressions?

First impressions are impressions that strangers form of you within the first few seconds of meeting you. Some call them *snapshots* or *polaroids*; some call them *thin slices*; yet others say it's *judging the book by its cover.*

They are a brief synopsis of the story that is *you* — enough to judge whether you are an adventure or political thriller, science fiction, romance, comedy or fantasy. That's enough for them to decide whether they want to know more about you or reject you right there. What they look for are facets like attractiveness, likability, trustworthiness, competence, aggressiveness and others depending on the situation.

If we compare you for the moment with a layer cake, strangers see a thin slice right into the centre of the cake that is you. They know the layers of chocolate, vanilla and butter in addition to the chocolate-vanilla bombs and nuts all at a glance. Coupled with a whiff of the chocolate, they have a strong impression of what stands in front of them.

Not only are first impressions quick to form, they last forever. Like the cake here, they are formed from the multiple facets of yourself that you display. Whether or not you are aware of it, at any given point in time, you have on display some facets. While a few may remain the same, others change with changing business, social or personal situations.

Based on these facets, strangers form quick first impressions and use them to derive conclusions about your overall personality. Statisticians might call it extrapolating. Doctors would call it a biopsy. For us, they are first impressions. Taking a few visible facets, we rapidly construct a personality sketch from them.

Question is, which of these facets do you display? Are you aware of the ones that you display? Is there more to you than the facets you currently display?

You may not be fully aware of all of the facets of your personality. Add to that the fact that you are not aware of all the facets that you display. As a result, some of your strengths remain hidden. At the same time, you may inadvertently display tiny weaknesses. Greater awareness helps you take control of what you display, giving the stranger the chance to form a powerful positive first impression of you.

In our capacity as manager, guide, business owners and consultants, we have worked with many people and have seen first impressions affecting their business, social and personal lives. They find it hard to believe when we explain that at a job interview, the time when they have to make an impact is the time it takes for them to say 'Hello', offer a handshake and make the opening comments. By now, their interviewers have already formed their first impressions of them.

Now tell us, did you really set the direction in your last interview?

If you had waited for the questions to begin, you had waited too long and didn't play a role in setting the direction.

First impressions are not limited to just formal interviews. Each person that you meet in your daily life — your colleagues, peers, strangers at a social event or during travel and within families — is forming a first impression of you. Sometimes, they have the power to make or break your job or marriage. At other times, they could be the silent observers who make you increasingly uncomfortable, make your tasks difficult and have the potential to stand in the way of your success and happiness. You owe it yourself to create powerful positive first impressions, because your success, happiness and fulfillment depends on them.

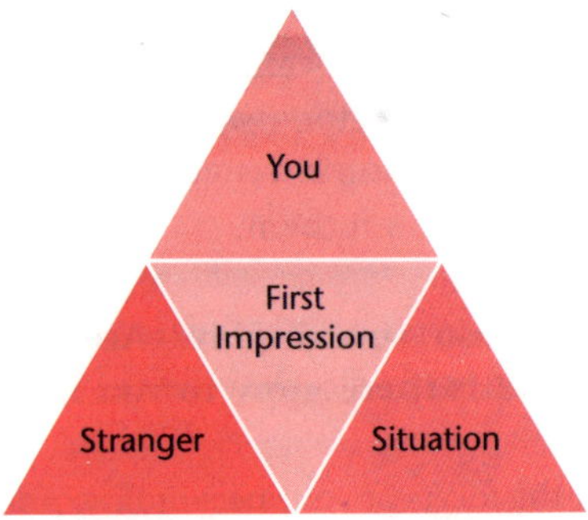

But, you may ask, how do I know what these strangers see in a first impression?

The answer lies first in the fact that every first impression is contextual. It is based on a *situation* where the strangers in front of you are trying to maximize pleasure or profit to themselves while minimizing pain or loss. Secondly, it depends on the *strangers'* perceptions, knowledge and experience. It is what the strangers consider important in the given situation and the characteristics they want to see in you and the way they see them. Thirdly, it depends on *you*.

The unforgiving thing about first impressions is that, once formed, they are imprinted on the brain practically forever, making them lasting impressions. Negative and weak first impressions carry a strong imprint.

Difficult to believe?

Each of us is forming first impressions every time we meet a stranger. While good impressions are long lasting, negative impressions are particularly tough to correct.

Take the example of Sanjay Singh when he met his future son-in-law for the first time. A feeling of instant disquiet settled on him and he found it hard to smile. Throughout dinner though, all was seemingly right and he couldn't find a reason for his discomfort. He tried to warn his daughter, or at the least, delay the marriage, get family and friends to speak to her. Nothing worked. His daughter knew her father's discomfort with the proposal, but put it down to routine parental objections and the marriage took place.

Sanjay tried hard to like his son-in-law for his daughter's sake, but a thin layer of carefully hidden discomfort remained.

One day, his wife asked him. "You never did take to him, did you?"

Sanjay was reluctant to pursue the subject.

"What did you see," his wife persisted, "that makes you so uncomfortable?"

"I don't know," said Sanjay. "It was just a feeling I had the moment I saw him."

"Ok, then why don't you think back? What about him didn't you like in the first meeting?" she asked.

A person may not always be able to articulate the reasons for the feeling or know the reasons behind the first impression. The hundreds of elements that our brains assess before coming to the snap judgment remain largely hidden from our conscious mind. But in this case, bits and pieces of the elements that added up to Sanjay Singh's first impression spilled out.

"What I recollect is a person who either didn't know enough or didn't

feel the meeting was important," said Sanjay, bringing up the image of the first encounter in his mind. "And I don't think it's because he didn't know. There we were, all set to welcome him home and he stood there in what I can only describe as completely casual attire. Too casual for an important dinner. He wasn't ready to meet us halfway either."

"What do you mean?" his wife was puzzled.

"He stood unbending," Sanjay struggled for the right words. "He just stood there, waiting for me to make the move. Not a hint of reaching out, not willing to bend or meet me halfway."

There were more, but these crucial elements determined Sanjay Singh's first impression in the first few seconds.

Isn't it unfair, you may question, particularly when negative impressions are formed? How can we say with certainty that first impressions are accurate?

Maybe it was your bad day. Or the interviewer's. Or she didn't read you well. Or didn't take the trouble to. In those few seconds, what could she know of you, the real you, your potential, your competence and your sincere intention to work hard?

But first, was Sanjay Singh correct in his views? Maybe there were circumstances beyond the future son-in-law's control that made him arrive in the casual attire. Maybe he was delayed at the office or on field work and chose to come rather than cancel the dinner which, he might have felt, would be rude. Maybe, he was nervous and jittery at the prospect of meeting his would-be in-laws and waited for the Singhs to take the lead.

There could be any number of reasons. But reality is, there was a sense that something was not quite right. A negative first impression was formed in what was to be a lifelong and important relationship when it could have been averted with enough preparation and proper communication.

Plenty of research is being carried out to understand how and why first impressions are formed and the kind of impressions that are formed in a given situation. But, it is the accuracy of first impressions that has undergone the most rigorous testing.

How Accurate are First Impressions?

Given the few seconds in which first impressions are formed, it is easy to question their accuracy. We can argue that as humans, we are complex beings. How can any single person consider all the elements that make up our persona and come to a snap judgment within seconds of laying eyes on us? Isn't that illogical? Doesn't that sound too simplistic?

The answer lies in these last two questions themselves. Certain parts of our brain form instant impressions and don't require the full details of the stranger's persona to come to a judgment. The mechanisms related to our survival in the jungle are valid even

HOW THE BRAIN FORMS RAPID FIRST IMPRESSIONS

Parts of our brain interact with one another in forming first impressions and storing the experience.

- Amygdala — The Amygdala is associated with a range of functions, including emotion, learning, memory, attention and perception. It processes positive and negative emotions, making judgments related to reward and fear[1] — whether an event, thing or person benefits us and whether it is a threat to us. Hence, it plays the primary role in forming first impressions. It is intuitive, seemingly effortless and automatic, relying on pre-existing knowledge and experience to extrapolate from the few facts disclosed. The Amygdala is also involved in the storage of events. It is believed that the stronger the emotional response to an event, the stronger the eventual memory storage of that event.

- Cerebral Cortex — The Cerebral Cortex is the most highly developed part of the brain and determines the cognitive and emotional functions. Conscious experience, including perceptions, emotions, thought and planning, in addition to many unconscious cognitive and emotional responses emerge from here[2]. It is the logical and analytical part of the brain that people mistakenly believe forms first impressions. It is based on reasoning and takes time because it takes into consideration all the facts necessary.
- Hippocampus — The Hippocampus plays an important role in the storage of information from short-term to long-term memory, adding to our body of knowledge and experience. When it comes to memories related to emotions, it works with the Amygdala in memory storage[3]. This stored knowledge and experience in turn will be drawn upon for future judgments, both in first impressions and logical thinking.

To sum up, the Amygdala forms instant first impressions based on past experience. Further, based on the Amygdala and its emotional response to the event, the Hippocampus stores the experience for reference in future events. Hence, it can easily be termed the cycle of first impressions, with past impressions and experience influencing the current ones and these in turn, influencing future impressions with another stranger.

today, when we have moved out into the civilized world. In addition to issues of physical survival, today, our brain also judges issues of social survival. The relevant parts of our brain take one quick glimpse of the key elements on display, bypass the logical processing areas and form the first impression within a few seconds. *(For details, see the box titled — How the Brain Forms Rapid First Impressions.)*

But again, are they accurate?

People are fairly accurate in forming their first impressions, according to researchers[4]. But, certain factors influence the accuracy of the impression. Some of us are easier to judge and some persons are better judges. Further, factors like the person's motivation can influence accuracy. Hence, there are times when first impressions miss the mark too.

Here, the question isn't how accurate these impressions are. The question is really, are they similar to the impressions formed after long interactions?

Studies conducted on groups of people from different walks of life in different situations have shown people forming first impressions within seconds without exception. These studies have also shown how these impressions stand the test of longer interactions.

So the premise that given enough time you can impress the stranger with your skills, competence and diligence may have little truth in it. Our advice is, create a powerful positive first impression within the first few seconds. Spend the rest of the interaction reinforcing it.

Consider one study where students rated teachers based on 10-second silent video clips. The correlation was extremely high between the students' ratings for each teacher with those of end-of-semester evaluations from actual students[5].

In yet another study[6], untrained people were shown 20 to 32-second video tapes of job applicants greeting interviewers. These people rated the applicants on self-assurance and likability. Their assessments were similar to those of the interviewers who had spent at least 20 minutes with each applicant.

But, you may ask, don't first impressions change in the course of future interactions, giving us a chance to repair poor first impressions?

The answer unfortunately, is "No", unless you make a deliberate effort to change the impression.

Consider the study[7] where first year students at a college were paired with another student of the same sex whom they had never met before. As per instructions, the students introduced themselves and spoke for 3, 6 or 10 minutes. After the conversation, they predicted their future relationship. Over the next nine weeks, they interacted normally with the rest of the students. At the end of the nine weeks, students who had rated each other positively had the closest friendships. It didn't matter whether the students sat together for 3, 6 or 10 minutes. It could have happened on first glance.

What happens then when you face multiple interviewers? Whose first impression is likely to be accurate?

Take the example of Kamlesh Sinha who was being interviewed for the position of General Manager-Weaving at a textile mill. Within moments, the Head of Human Resources, who was conducting the interview, rated Kamlesh high on trustworthiness and as a group player, both extremely valued traits for the position he was being interviewed for.

Let's recap for a moment the fact that first impressions are a product of the situation, the stranger and yourself. In a different company or with a different interviewer, being an individual player and a go-getter may hold higher value.

When the Business Unit Head interviewed Kamlesh, it was with great reluctance that he gave the go-ahead. The factor that forced him was shortage of candidates with suitable technical skills. To help him introduce modern systems and processes, the Unit Head had been looking for a person experienced in the current corporate world rather than one from the traditional industry.

Here, the question isn't whether the HR Head was right or the Business Unit Head was. Question is whether Kamlesh could do the work as per requirement and manage the people effectively. The important question for Kamlesh is, what first impressions did he leave on his interviewers?

If the impression he created with the HR Head wasn't positive, he wouldn't get past the first hurdle. If the impression he created with the Unit Head was not positive, he is likely to have a less than positive relationship with his boss. Not an ideal situation to work in.

When multiple interviewers are involved, which is often the case not only in companies but also in our personal lives, perceptions of each interviewer may differ. The facets of your personality that you display must be based on these differing perceptions. As far as technical skills are concerned, there is likely to be little dispute. Differences crop up in how the interviewers perceive facets like attractiveness, likability, trustworthiness, competence, aggressiveness and the importance they ascribe to them.

This advice holds good for your personal life too. That the prospective bride has made a good impression on the prospective groom may only be half the job done. Factor in the mother-in-law, sisters-in-law, father-in-law and others, and you realize that many more positive first impressions must be created before she can say that she has taken the right first steps. It is because, eventually families do influence how happy you are with your spouse.

So, rather than concern ourselves with whether the stranger's first impressions are accurate, it is more practical to understand why and how we form first impressions.

Why Do We Form First Impressions?

When we humans lived in the jungle, a first impression made the difference between life and death everyday of our lives. With a wild animal staring down at us, it would never have occurred to us to ask the question, even if we knew how to — "Why do we form first impressions in the first place?"

Life was straightforward and the rules for staying alive were simple. Stay on the lookout, take note of the predator, watch its mood, get out of its way, stay alive. Or track the herd, identify the weakling, attack, get your meal. We call this the question of — *What does the elephant mean to me?*

Image 2

Let's take a hypothetical instance in the jungle. Imagine for a moment that you are lost in a jungle. After wandering for a long time, you found yourself stepping out into a familiar clearing. All you need to do is cross the clearing to reach your tribe on the other side. But, in the clearing is a herd of elephants. The sun is setting already and you want to reach your tribe by nightfall.

Image 1

Standing closest to you are two elephants, part of the herd that is otherwise grazing peacefully farther away. Your safety depends on how quickly you can decide whether these two elephants are dangerous or not.

Quick! Give your First Impression!

Safe, you'd think. More likely than not, you'd say that Image 1 is not intrinsically harmful, a playful baby elephant in fact. In those few seconds, you decide it's a safe one. You could skirt the herd a bit and make your way out of the clearing in the most non-threatening manner.

You are now a few steps out in the clearing and at a point closest to the baby elephant. The second elephant (Image 2) lifts its head, its ears stand out and with a loud trumpet, charges at you.

Snap judgment. What do you decide?

Mother's out to guard its young one, you'd think. Your instinctive reaction is to step back into the forest, maybe even climb a sturdy tree for the night until the herd moves on. You would not risk your life with this angry elephant.

What was happening here? First, you identify that it's an elephant. It's worth your life paying attention to it. Faced with a rabbit, you are likely to ignore it and go on your way. Second, your brain is simultaneously looking through the information it holds related to experience and knowledge of an elephant's nature. Three, you notice its size, body language, its trumpet, map it against the knowledge in your head and make a snap judgment of its intent. An instant decision based on a first impression.

Would you rather continue across the clearing and experience the elephant before you decide whether it is in fact of danger to you?

That's madness. So for your own protection, your brain is wired to take those instant snapshots of the situation, person and background and come to a life-saving conclusion.

This might be a straight forward and obvious example, but in our everyday lives, we make hundreds of similar snap judgments to predict what the strangers we meet mean to us. It is the same as the jungle question — *What does the elephant mean to me?*

At the basic survival level, we answer these types of questions — Does he intend harm? Does she mean to be selfish? Is he going to be open and trustworthy? Will she lend a helping hand?

At a more complex level, we answer these questions — Is he

aggressive enough for the company? Conversely, is she too aggressive for the company? Does he fit into my company, family, social circle?

What's necessary in the wild jungle is necessary in the human jungle we live in today. Only the mechanism varies given that it is a different set of things that we need to identify and assess. We may have a fair semblance of security from brutal life and death situations, although we do have to guard against them occasionally. But, more common are the daily instances of meeting strangers who bring us success, comfort and happiness or those who bring us pain, loss and unhappiness.

But what, you may ask, does the jungle have to do with staying happy, comfortable and successful?

To achieve these objectives, the basic principle of the jungle continues to be relevant — take a thin slice and form rapid first impressions. The single largest difference from the jungle is that the fabric of human life today is not so much of living and dying, but of maximizing positive outcomes and minimizing negative outcomes and of living happily within our tribes.

In the wild jungle, the question of *What does the elephant mean to me* is a matter of physical survival. It's pure action. But in the human jungle, the role of survival is also a question of reward and fear. The basic objective remains the same — survival. It's just that the terms of survival differ.

Think of the dozens of people who cross our paths in a day. Even in the fleeting interactions where we pass by strangers on the road, we form a rapid first impression to decide whether to go on our straight path, to take an aggressive stance, smile, or simply move away. With close and long-term interactions, we look for more than that. We predict the more complex outcome of whether we can have a business, social or personal relationship with them. If we decide that we can have one with them, we go a step further to decide the potential strength of the relationship. This is the means to survival in the human jungle.

Is there more to first impressions than personal benefit?
We are social beings, living in close proximity in a highly networked world, both physically and virtually. Our every move and micro-move is read, processed and interpreted continuously by strangers around us, whether or not we actually interact with them. And their impressions of us affect them too since all of us are part of a social fabric.

How does a stranger's first impression affect you?
Imagine an abrasive driver who has changed lanes abruptly, ramming into the car in the right lane. He gets out and is haranguing the other driver who is not at fault. Feelings of disquiet, anger, impotence, in addition to sympathy for the other driver, all clash at their negative best to occupy your brain space. That's black ink on your emotions.

Now, imagine the man who gives up his seat in the bus so that the tired mother, carrying her baby and a heavy bag, can sit. A smile appears on your face. This act of kindness and empathy eases your heart and your feelings come together at their positive best to occupy your brain space. That's white ink on your emotions.

First impressions of the people around us affect us, our personal happiness, our social inclusiveness and our professional success positively or negatively. Similarly, the first impressions we create in other people's minds, affect them too. Still, knowing the importance of first impressions is not enough to create powerful positive first impressions. The question of how first impressions are formed becomes crucial for us to take a step forward.

How are First Impressions Formed?

The question of how first impressions are formed cannot be

answered completely without recognizing our own *goals* when we meet strangers, the *repercussions* of first impressions and what we do with the fresh *information gathered.*

What are our *goals*? What do we try to predict?

First and foremost, the ability to create positive first impressions depends on our goal of maximizing positive outcomes and minimizing negative outcomes. To meet this goal, we try to predict the future outcome or relationship with the stranger. This is the Predicted Outcome Value Theory at play, introduced by Professor Michael Sunnafrank[8]. The theory is true for business, social or personal relationships.

The actual facets that we look for in the stranger to meet our goal differ with different situations. For example, the facets you are likely to look for in a sales executive would be aggression, high social confidence and goal-orientation. On the other hand, the facets you look for in a friend could be patience and empathy. These goals play a strong role in the first impressions you form. They in turn, influence the repercussions of first impressions.

What are the *repercussions* once first impressions are formed?

Repercussions of first impressions are serious and long lasting. Not only do strangers proceed to confirm the positive first impressions, they also form positive lasting impressions. Simultaneously, they mirror the facets they see and extrapolate from these facets to create a prototype of your entire personality in their mind.

A. Confirmation of First Impressions

Once a first impression is formed, interviewers no longer take a neutral view to assess you. On the contrary, they proceed with the interview to validate the first impressions already formed. If the interviewer has formed a negative impression that you are mild and unable to stand up for yourself, their line of questioning will follow to confirm that impression. It is up to you to bring in damage control and show your positive facets while playing down this facet.

B. Self-fulfilling Prophecy and Lasting Impressions

As discussed earlier, research[9] shows that students, once they form a positive impression of the student next to them, ended up creating a positive relationship with them in the next nine months.

What the students were doing was to predict rapidly whether a future relationship was possible and hence, whether it was worth investing their time and effort in creating that relationship.

This was part of the research carried out by Professor Michael Sunnafrank and Art Ramirez to prove the Predicted Outcome Value Theory[10]. As per the theory, we determine the benefit of the relationship by predicting the value of future outcomes, whether positive or negative[11]. Hence, we are maximizing the benefit to ourselves and minimizing the pain in making the snap judgment.

Professor Sunnafrank's research also revealed the self-fulfilling prophecy at work[12]. When we predict the kind of future relationship we are likely to have with the person, we are determining the effort we shall put into developing the relationship. When we form a positive first impression of the person, we are more open to the person and invest our time and effort in creating the relationship that we predicted. On the other hand, if it was a negative first impression, we close ourselves to the person and limit our interaction, giving no chance for the relationship to form. The first impression then solidifies into a negative lasting impression.

C. Mirror Effect

Related to the self-fulfilling prophecy is the mirror effect brought about by our brain's mirror neurons (*For detailed explanation, see the box titled Mirror Neurons)*. What is the Mirror Effect? You see a stranger stub her toe against the bed post, you flinch instinctively. You see the hero of the movie thrash the villain and your muscles tense with the action. Mirror neurons are behind this instinctive action wherein we mirror the mood of other people[13].

Not only are strangers forming a first impression of you, they are also responding to that impression. It might be as simple as a smile that disappears or conversely, an interview that takes a positive line, depending on the first impression formed. For instance, if your demeanour is viewed as one of pride and arrogance, we may see interviewers mirroring it overtly or covertly through their own responses and line of questioning.

D. Extrapolation to Other Areas — Comprehensive Impressions

Once strangers form a first impression, they extrapolate this to other areas of your persona, creating a halo effect. On the basis of just a few visible facets, a prototype of your entire personality is created in their mind. In doing so, the extrapolation creates a comprehensive view for them. Let us suppose that you turn yourself out neat and organized and greet the stranger with an open engaging smile. Firstly, she is likely to decide that you are a well-meaning, likable person and this impression stays with her forever. Secondly, she extrapolates this bit of data to come to the conclusion that you behave in this fashion in all the other areas of your life. Thus, a comprehensive impression is formed.

MIRROR NEURONS

Mirror neurons are a special class of brain cells that fire not only when an individual performs an action, but also when the individual observes someone else make the same movement. We understand others not by thinking, but by feeling. Mirror neurons appear to let us 'simulate' not just other people's actions, but the intentions and emotions behind those actions[14].

Trouble is, what's true of us in the current situation may not be true for other areas. Take the following example to see how it works:

Sunita is a good leader and manager of her twelve-member regional marketing team. She has hands-on experience, an approachable nature and is a group player who happens to be an introvert. She makes it a point to attend the company's social events for her team's sake as well as for the informal chats with peers and superiors. Yet, she is happy to let her team take centre stage and after a round of socializing, is one of the early ones to leave.

On one such occasion, the new HR manager from the head office who had put in a late appearance at the event felt Sunita lacked in approachability. He construed her lack of overt exuberance as a reluctance to mingle with the crowd. He drew the conclusion that there was a strong element of arrogance to her. This was accentuated by the fact that due to his late appearance, by the time he reached her, she was on the point of leaving. After a brief exchange of courtesies, she had bid her good bye.

When he moved on to a different company and was looking for a marketing manager, Sunita's name came up for discussion. But, he held his reservations and eventually Sunita was not considered although her work reviews were excellent. The HR manager had viewed the thin slice of Sunita at a social occasion where her behaviour didn't fit with his perception that a marketing manager must be ready to mingle and carry visible interest in people. He extrapolated it to mean arrogance and a reluctance to work with people at all levels.

Many times, people do get carried away by the thin slices of us in remotely related situations and it is for us to be cautious about such first impressions.

Now, that the repercussions are clear, what do we do with this *fresh information gathered?*

Each piece of knowledge and every experience is stored in our long-term memory. The stronger our emotional response to an event, the stronger is the memory. It is like the child who once got burnt while playing with matches, never touching a match again.

Even as first and lasting impressions are formed, the experience is added to our body of knowledge and experience. This in turn will be drawn upon for future judgments.

Given all these elements, creating powerful positive first impressions is an art and a science. While it is important to learn the principles behind the science, perceiving the stranger in front accurately and applying the principles to generate powerful positive impressions is the art behind the science.

Repercussions of First Impressions

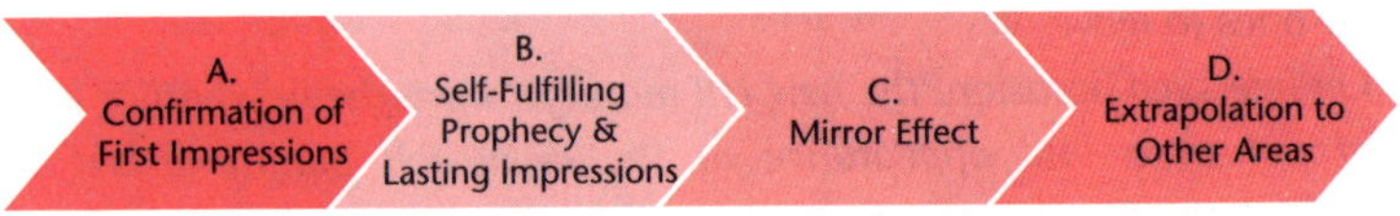

REFERENCES

1 The Amygdala and Reward, by Mark G. Baxter and Elisabeth A.Murray - http://lnpsych.nimh.nih.gov/murray/nat.rev.neurosci.pdf

2 The Human Brain - http://www.learner.org/discoveringpsychology/brain/brain_flash.html

3 Human emotion and memory: interactions of the amygdala and hippocampal complex, by Elizabeth A.Phelps - http://psych.nyu.edu/phelpslab/papers/04_CON_V14.pdf

4 Do We Know When Our Impressions of Others Are Valid? Evidence for Realistic Accuracy Awareness in First Impressions of Personality By Biesanz, Human, Paquin, Chan, Parisotto, Sarracino and Gillis - http://spp.sagepub.com/content/2/5/452.full.pdf+html

5 http://www.apa.org/monitor/mar05/slices.aspx

6 http://www.psychologytoday.com/articles/200405/the-first-impression

7 http://abcnews.go.com/Technology/story?id=69942&page=1#.TsZxsd6lm0s - Journal of Social and Personal Relationships - http://www.webmd.com/balance/news/20040910/first-impressions-guide-relationships

8 http://www.d.umn.edu/comm/facultystaff/msunnafrank.php

9 http://abcnews.go.com/Technology/story?id=69942&page=1#.TsZxsd6lm0s - Journal of Social and Personal Relationships - http://www.webmd.com/balance/news/20040910/first-impressions-guide-relationships

10 http://abcnews.go.com/Technology/story?id=69942&page=1#.T-2MUrW_HkV

11 http://faculty.evansville.edu/dt4/301/primer301.html

12 http://www.webmd.com/balance/news/20040910/first-impressions-guide-relationships

13 Brain Briefings: November 2008. Society for Neuroscience - http://www.sfn.org/siteobjects/published/0000BDF20016F63800FD712C30FA42DD/299BC9518D9BED4789B6A3ABFBE5DFA4/file/BB_mirror_neurons.pdf

14 http://www.sfn.org/siteobjects/published/0000BDF20016F63800FD712C30FA42DD/299BC9518D9BED4789B6A3ABFBE5DFA4/file/BB_mirror_neurons.pdf

SO FAR

- First impressions form within seconds.
- They are formed from the multiple elements that you display each moment of your life.
- First impressions are extrapolated to other areas of personality to create comprehensive impressions.
- First impressions are self-fulfilling prophecies and create lasting impressions.
- First impressions are a factor of you, the stranger and the situation.
- Once formed, further interactions are used to confirm the first impressions.
- First impressions were found to reflect impressions formed at the end of long interactions.
- When multiple interviewers are involved, it is necessary to create powerful positive first impressions on each one of them.

- *What does the elephant mean to me?* We make a prediction of the outcome of every interaction with a stranger based on our goals.
- We take a thin slice and form first impressions to maximize positive outcomes and minimize negative outcomes.
- The body of knowledge and experience of the event is added to the long-term memory based on the emotional impact.

Chapter 2

Many Lives, Many Applications

Seeing yourself as you want to be is the key to personal growth.

— Unknown

A cat has nine lives, so they say.

How many lives do we have?

Before you answer that it is a meaningless question unless you believed in the theory of karma, hear us out. We do live many lives, sometimes in a single day. We wake up to our personal life, move on to our business life and the occasional social life at the end of the day while we could be carrying on a parallel virtual life that comprises our business, social and personal circles throughout the day.

The sum total of these and other lives is a single lifetime of ours. What we do with these lives determines our success, happiness and what we achieve in our lifetime. Sometimes, success in one life makes up for indifferent performance in another. It all depends on how important that life is to us. For Smita, her work with charities gave meaning to her life and made up for the niggling troubles in her personal life with in-laws who had never accepted her.

Like a full course meal that can be had in a few different ways, your life is yours to make what you want of it. Whether you want your business life to be your main course, the personal life the perfect dessert and your social life the occasional wine that adds flavour to your life or the other way round, it's up to you to rearrange your lives based on your preferences, goals, priorities and of course, the constraints.

But, what do first impressions have to do with these lives?
To live in human society means to live by complex rules and rituals. First impressions are about meeting the rules that govern the many lives. Some of these rules are left unsaid while some are well laid down. What we want out of each life decides the rules by which we live and hence the first impressions we create. These impressions in turn determine whether we get what we want in our lives and ultimately our success and happiness.

Depending on the life we are leading at a given point in time, there are rules and guidelines as to how we clothe and groom ourselves, how we conduct ourselves, what we speak and how we speak. Our advice is to remain conscious of our different lives and the guiding principles behind each since the repercussions are deep and long lasting.

So what are these different lives that we live?
There are seven lives which broadly cover our lifetime, each having rules, guidelines, rituals and objectives of its own.

1. Inner Life
2. Personal Life
3. Social Life
4. Business Life
5. Virtual Life
6. Transient Life
7. Public Life

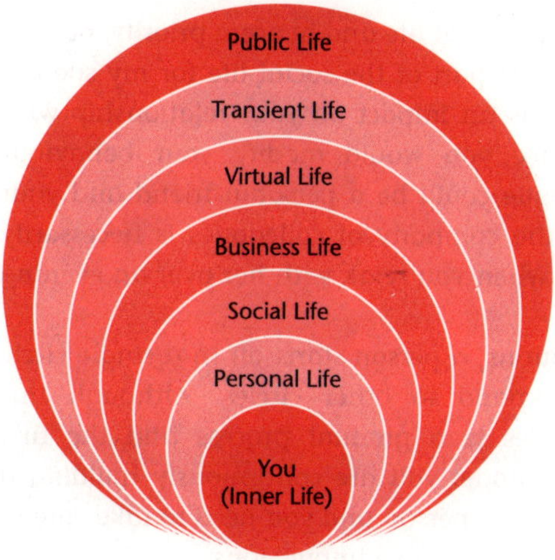

Before we go into each of these lives and what makes them tick, it is important to note that there are as many variations within each of these lives as there are among trees. There are trees with thick, strong trunks and widespread branches like a mango tree and those with lean and long trunks without a spot of shade for passersby like a eucalyptus. Then there are those with leaves that turn orange and shed during autumn like an oak and those that are green through the year like a neem tree.

Similarly, no person's life in one area remains the same as that of another person's. Your business life might be entirely different in meaning, content and outlook compared to that of your colleague. Taking this a step further, where a person belongs in one of your lives isn't sacrosanct. Some people belong to a single circle. For example, a colleague from the office with whom you have a strictly work relationship may not belong to the other circles of your life. But, others may have overlapping lives with you. For example, you may develop a friendship with another colleague and this person may be present in your business, social and personal circles. Or your spouse might be your business partner too and hence would be present in all three circles.

The placement of people in a circle also affects your relationship with others in the circle because your demands, priorities and behaviour differ in their presence. For instance, I have a close friend who is part of my personal life and hence a priority, but the same friend is probably just part of the social life for my spouse. Each such relationship has an impact on your relationship with others in the circle since you would modify your behaviour accordingly. Or a colleague could be a personal friend and your behaviour with her in the company of colleagues is necessarily different from what it is when you relax with her over an evening cup of tea.

Firstly, with few exceptions, a person starts off in a single circle and may eventually expand to other circles. Although this stepping into other circles is a gradual process and the first impressions are already made, you are continuously building a new set of equations with this person and you need to take care to sustain and build upon those positive impressions.

Secondly, depending on the importance of a certain life and the changes that take place over time in this life, the first impressions you need to create change. Let's take for example a promotion from the position of an assistant to that of a manager. The first impressions you now create would be not just your technical capability and ability to handle the task diligently, but how you manage your team, your new bosses and peers too. Similarly, a new set of first impressions are created when a new member enters your family, such as a new sister-in-law or brother-in-law.

Thirdly, you may have fleeting or long-term relationships, superficial or strong relationships, shared or highly personal relationships. And that is as it should be. What matters is that you make the appropriate first impressions in each life circle, depending on the type of relationship you hope to build.

Why is the nature of these relationships important when creating first impressions?

We tend to behave in a fashion that mirrors the role models around us, the strongest person in the crowd or the person with whom we feel a kinship. It's the mirror effect that we talked about in Chapter-1. It is easy at these times to get carried away, forgetting that other members are watching us. Sometimes it's from the sidelines. Other times it's from the thick of the action. Regardless, they are forming their first impressions and extrapolating it to relate to an entirely different life circle.

The rule is, when in private create the impression you need to on the person in front. When in public or with more than one person, create the impression you need to with the crowd at large. A word of caution though. It isn't about showing a different face each time. It is the degree of warmth, openness and empathy that you show that differs, not you as a person.

As we move seamlessly from one life circle to another, don't think for a moment that it is enough for you to behave in a uniform manner across all your lives and still create positive first impressions in each. It is equally untrue that you can behave in a completely opposite fashion with different people and not face some repercussions. What is true in one life easily spills over into the next. You can't be polite to your colleagues at an official lunch in a restaurant, while being rude to the waiter. You can't be great at your business life, being

empathetic and guiding your team mates while remaining indifferent at home. Nor can you be negative in your outlook at the office while being completely positive at home. Essentially, you cannot contradict yourself among the different lives.

You cannot be Dr Jekyll in one life and Mr Hyde in another. If you do that, you lose all equity that you hope to build. The place where it all begins is in your inner life. When perception is reality, you need to make your inner reality an outer perception for others. It is 'image from the inside out.'

DR JEKYLL AND MR HYDE

Written by RL Stevenson, the story is about Dr Jekyll who takes a potion which turns him from a mild-mannered person into the homicidal maniac, Mr Hyde. The story is associated with split personality disorder where a single person has two or more personalities living within the same body.

1. Inner Life

First, there exists the you with your inner life deep inside the privacy of your being, where you hold your personality, your thoughts, feelings, preferences, opinions, moods and inclinations.

But that is me, you might say. Is that a life by itself?

Yes, definitely. Each of us has an inner life. This life is what we present consciously or unconsciously to the outside world through our outer life.

We may present different facets to different people. Hence, we live multiple outer lives in different situations.

The inner life is where it all begins. Take a tree for instance. Our inner life is akin to the roots hidden deep inside the ground, supporting the plant's outer life — the trunk, branches, leaves, flowers, the fruits and the seed. If your inner life is strong, so will your outer lives be. On the other hand, if there is consistent trouble in one or more of your outer lives, it is time to take a deep, long look at your inner life.

So, what is this inner life?

The inner life is the sum total of the following:

1. *Who you are — Which you know*
2. *Who you are — Which you don't know*
3. *Who you could be*

These three aspects make up your inner life. Flowing across these aspects of your inner life is what others know of you. Sometimes, people can see some parts of you, but not other parts. At other times, they see parts that don't exist. In either case, it is for you to be aware of what people see in you and make adjustments to what you disclose accordingly — to show the positive parts that they can't see at a glance and play down a negative part that isn't relevant to the work at hand so that it doesn't distort their first impression unnecessarily.

Being aware of yourself inside out, knowing your potential and believing in that potential is the first step towards creating powerful positive first impressions. Your inner life ultimately reflects in your outer lives.

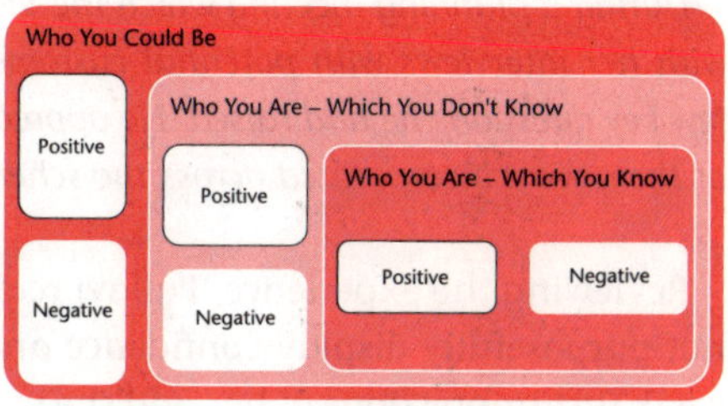

Inner Life

The real question is: Are you taking the time and effort to disclose this 'inner you' accurately to the outer world?

Pallavi was a diligent worker and an excellent architect. But, in contrast to her seemingly confident and more vocal team mates, she lacked a confident demeanour and was subdued in meetings. The result was that, despite her two years in the company, Pallavi was not noticed beyond her own team members and manager.

A change in bosses didn't help matters. Just as her earlier project manager was beginning to understand and value her potential, he moved to another company.

It was when one of her team mates was promoted to the position of senior architect that Pallavi sat down to think about where she was headed and what was going wrong. Despite her contribution and her capability, she had been overlooked.

She decided to make a fresh start. The opportunity came up soon enough. Pallavi was part of the team of architects that were to design the new high-end housing project meant to be a gated community.

Although she and her team were being led by their project manager, this was a prestigious project and the Vice-President of Projects himself was taking special interest in it.

Rather than depend on the briefing and her theoretical understanding of what a gated community requires, she spent time talking extensively to potential house buyers, observed them and their life style and made a list of key elements that would be important to them.

During a planning meeting which the Vice-President attended, backed with her interviews with potential customers, Pallavi had answers to a few key questions he had raised. He appreciated the inputs and a couple of them were incorporated across the scheme.

Reviewing the experience, Pallavi realized that as long as she did not purposefully display confidence and capability, people carried weak first impressions of her and she was ignored. It took longer for even her boss to understand her potential and when it came to other teams and the higher-ups, they simply did not see her potential. Stepping up her efforts allowed her to discover a more confident side to herself and display this with her work excellence to those beyond her team where it had an impact.

At this point, you may ask, isn't it a long stretch managing so many lives each day based on a single inner life?

The important thing is that your inner life determines which of your outer lives take precedence over others. Every one of your lives does not hold the same importance to you. While to some, their business life is the critical one, to others it is their personal, social or public lives. Yet others might be living in a virtual life.

It is your nature, preference and affinity to a certain life that determine the position of each life in your list of priorities. The important thing is to assess yourself to see what each life means to you and hence prioritize your action. Your efforts accordingly, will focus more on certain lives than on others.

But remember, what is critical at one stage of your life may change altogether at a different stage. With traumatic events like the death of a loved one or prolonged distress to family, indifferent business lives or simply getting on in years, there are many times when we need to re-evaluate our priorities.

In the end, the inner life being the core of all our lives determines the different lives and hence, our lifetime.

2. Personal Life

As much as we may believe that 'marriages are made in heaven', we may also believe with greater interest in 'love at first sight'. How does this happen?

In research conducted with fruit flies, females were biologically tuned to identify males which are genetically more compatible with them. When they mate with good matches, they produce more eggs, but when they mate with less compatible matches, the number is far less[1]. Researchers believe that this has meaning for humans as well.

Whether we really are like the fruit flies in finding our mates or it's a more emotional state than a purely biological state, fact is we decide fast whether or not we have found a person of interest. In research, it was found that men view women they are interested in for about 8.5 seconds. But if they look away in 4.5 seconds, then they are not interested[2]. That's a quick call.

Take speed dating where dozens of singles meet others for quick dates that don't last more than a few minutes, sometimes just three minutes. The idea is based on the reality that first impressions are accurate and speed dating is, therefore, catching on.

Before you discard the notion of speed dating as a product of the West, think about the senior marriage melas and senior live-in melas that are taking place across the cities of India[3]. As one participant who found a partner says, "When I saw her, there were butterflies in my stomach."

First impressions are at work here. This is as Karan says, "She walked into my office and I was supposed to interview her. I was intrigued from the beginning. Of course, we had the interview and although we were ready to recruit her because of her strong credentials, she finally chose not to join our company. Smitten is the only word I could use to describe what went on within. It's just as well that she didn't join, company policy and all that, made life simpler. We are together now," he smiles.

While every one of us may not have those 'love at first sight' moments, we do form those critical first impressions about potential spouses, just as the same potential spouse is forming first impressions about us.

Then again, while finding a life partner is one very important aspect of your personal life, think of the family members involved. Considering that positive relationships with in-laws play an important role in keeping families closely bonded, it is important that you do what it takes to create the necessary positive first impressions with in-laws too.

What is important is that, first impressions in your personal life are not limited to yourself. When you have children, as a parent, it becomes your concern to observe the first impressions your child or teen is creating and coach them with patience. After all, it is at home that children learn how to conduct themselves. Your children's lives become part of your personal life as well.

What care, therefore, do you take to help your children out in their lives?

Where children are concerned, first impressions are partly a matter of learning from example and partly based on the child's nature. While you work at creating strong and positive first impressions in your lives, ask yourself from time to time about the impressions your child needs to create and whether you are setting a good example for them. Whether you have conversations with them in which you listen and explain or share a good moment together, or whether you are there to support them, their personal lives are your concern.

3. Business Life

For those of you working in entities that have established systems and structure, like the corporate world, healthcare institutions, government departments, academic institutions and the like, the existing workforce serve as role models. By their very attire, grooming and behaviour, they show the rules of their world.

Whether you hold a trainee, middle management, or senior executive profile, the rules to create first impressions change. At each level, you have role models that you can emulate.

You may belong to the most stringent finance and legal industries or pharmaceutical and manufacturing industries or service industries like airlines, hospitality and retail or you may belong to the creative fields like advertising, film or music industries. Depending on the industry you work in, cultures differ and hence the rules by which you are judged will differ. Yet, with plenty of role models ahead of them, a person paying attention to the intricacies of the rules catches on fast and is carried along with the stream, creating positive first impressions.

But you may say, all I need to do is be professional in my demeanour and work ethic. If I achieve that, how can first impressions go wrong whatever the industry I am in?

But they do differ and rightly so. Each industry serves a specific purpose. Accordingly, it carries a different set of goals and objectives. In fact, it deals with an entirely different set of customers or enters different lives of the same customers. The result of this difference is that expectations vary and the capabilities they look for in their people differ. So do the people these industries employ. A different set of rules and guiding principles come into play in creating powerful first impressions. You need to understand the nuances of each industry in addition to being professional in your demeanour.

Hence, not only does the type of culture you must fit into differ from industry to industry, it can differ from department to department and at different levels of the hierarchy. For example, when Ashish moved up from being a senior support executive in a software company to the position of a manager, the company put him through a course that coached him on how to look the part of a manager in addition to guidance for the new level of responsibility.

Managerial impressions are different from technical impressions. Senior executive impressions are vastly different from mid-level impressions. What management looks for in factory personnel differs from that of service personnel and again from that of sales personnel. All these differ completely from that of finance personnel. When it comes to creative personnel, it's as if they live in a different world where the rules of the regular corporate world don't apply.

Companies may look for orderliness, attention to detail and timeliness in factory personnel, patience and an ability to handle customers of all kinds with a pleasant demeanour in service personnel. None of the rules that apply to these people may apply to creative personnel. Hence, identifying the industry and department you are in and looking for role models in them becomes essential. Because, you will be judged by the first impression you create based on the role you take upon yourself.

So, whether you have grown up with role models around you or you are from a place with none in your family or acquaintances being in the industry, find a role model to emulate. Doing the wrong thing at the wrong time can put your audience off.

4. Social Life

Overlapping with the rest of your lives is your social life where you meet not only people from the personal or business lives, but also strangers and acquaintances. While social etiquette demands adherence to certain broad rules, the rules themselves depend on the kind of social life you find yourself in.

Do you find yourself in formal corporate events, casual corporate events, personal gatherings, celebrations like New Year, Christmas or Diwali or are we talking of charity events, book launches or music celebrations?

There are as many types of events as there seem to be shades of colour in our world. Each of them and your deportment at these events mark your social life as well as a permanent tattoo does. This tattoo also determines the first impressions you create within your social life. Yet, at each of these events, the rules governing first impressions differ.

To create the right impression, are you doing the right thing at the different social events?

From dress code to timeliness to dining etiquette, there are plenty of rules for social events. The more formal the event, the more well-defined the rules are. It pays to learn the spoken as well as the unspoken rules.

The dangerous thing about your social life is that you are probably at your most open, unwary best, letting your hair down and having a great time. But watch out. There are plenty of examples of potential employers, friends and life partners or their families meeting people at a social event and forming their first impressions when the person is totally unaware and least prepared for it. It is common knowledge that people attend marriages on the lookout for spouses for their children. So, while the assumed purpose of a social event may be one thing, the real purpose might be entirely different, at least for some.

This is the point where trouble begins if you are not prepared for it. You might be at your social best and what people see of this social side of you can give them a wrong impression of what you really are like in your other lives.

So, while we do not advise you to be constantly wary, we do suggest that you give some thought to your other lives when you are at a social event.

On the good side, social events that are an offshoot of your business or personal lives pave a great way to resolve office or family issues. They are also good ice-breakers when welcoming new members into the fold, giving you the chance to create positive first impressions in a relaxed environment with little pressure. This is why organizations often make it a point of having semi-casual dinners and off-site conferences. They are looking for occasions to get together for congratulations on projects or personal achievements as well as occasions for farewells and welcome to new entrants or visiting executives.

What is the best way to create positive first impressions at a social event?

To make the most of these social events, you ought to be able to shed some part of your business behaviour and be at ease. More importantly, put other people at ease and you can build closer relationships or make up for strained office relations. If you are a spouse attending the office party, the positive first impression you create reflects on your spouse's image and success. It is as much your responsibility as his.

When it comes to social gatherings for family or friends, it can be a time to renew acquaintances, so that your personal social fabric remains strong. Given the proximity of families, first impressions with these acquaintances can have a positive effect on you and close family members and hence must be handled with warmth, politeness and kinship.

Today, when many of you live far from family members, in different cities and countries, the community you live in becomes your social life. It is common for the societies you live in to organize a range of events from festivals to New Year parties, helping you create a strong, social fabric wherever you live. Creating positive first impressions continuously is as important as when you are new to the place. As old families leave and new families move in over time, it makes sense to continue to create positive first impressions with one's neighbours.

After all, when there's an emergency, it is neighbours who take care of things at the first sign of trouble even before family or friends arrive. When Akshat's father had a heart attack, it was his neighbours who rushed the ailing gentleman to hospital and took care of things until relatives came to lend a helping hand. Your neighbourhood is your small village, so create great impressions and sustain them.

5. Virtual Life

The most significant addition to our lives in this century are our virtual lives, the lives we live via Facebook, e-mail, chat, blogs, comments, forums, discussion boards and the innumerable communities that we belong to, creating an online life for ourselves.

Overlapping with your physical lives, yet retaining the world that it calls its own, virtual lives have a real and strong impact on all your physical lives. They often create a first impression well before you meet the strangers in person.

Future life partners and their families, business partners, even casual acquaintances are checking you out on social media both before and after meeting you. And they are willing to reassess their readiness to form a relationship with you based on your virtual life.

What is the virtual image that you project? Who are your friends? Where are you present? What do your posts and comments signify?

Each word that you put on the Internet builds your profile, comment by comment, post by post, and can be traced, making its way back to you.

In addition to traditional modes of background checks, many companies are now making social media background checks compulsory. Not only does this tell them the basics about you, it is also a mechanism to make sure that there are no skeletons in your cupboard. Long before you sit face to face with the interviewers, they have formed a first impression of you, albeit a virtual one. It's the hidden threshold you need to cross after your resume clears its mark.

All looked good on Sheena's resume. As senior customer care executive at an e-commerce portal, she was capable, knew her domain and was unfailingly courteous to the rudest of customers. Yet, a stray comment posted on a day when a customer had given her a bad time on the phone came back to haunt her. She was never called for an interview for the job she had applied for.

Or take the case of Sakshi for instance. At a friend's New Year party, she stood chatting with a group of friends when a stranger was introduced by the host. Project manager at a software company, he was quick with his wit and ready with a smile. Sakshi found herself drawn to him and eventually they found themselves talking to each other about everything and nothing.

It was nothing at all like a conversation with a stranger. They were so much at ease with each other. When finally, they exchanged numbers, Facebook IDs and mail addresses and Sakshi left for home, she had a smile on her face.

The first thing she did was check him on Facebook and what does she see? His comments in a thread to a particularly derogatory post about an actress gave her a glimpse of the nasty turn his wit could take. Disliking a person, even if it was a public figure like an actress, was not cause enough to post comments that bordered on the demeaning. Not something Sakshi could endorse.

Mr Right suddenly didn't seem so right any more. Sakshi never accepted his friend request, nor did she return his calls or e-mails. An end to a potential relationship.

6. Transient Life

Falling in the realm of your transient life is your life where you meet strangers for the first and possibly the last time. It is the battery of people who are distant acquaintances, service executives offering their services to us or just plain strangers passing by us on the road, rail or flight.

While first impressions formed in the course of your business, personal, social, virtual and public lives have great impact on your lives, those with strangers and service executives don't get

the same attention and importance. You could ask, after all what has a stranger got to do with my life? What do the first impressions I create have to do with a service executive whom I see once in my life time or in a year?

Sometimes, the answer is because you never know who the stranger might turn out to be. But the bigger answer is, because behind every stranger lies a human.

Consider a stranger on the road. How many times has a stranger on the road come to your aid, or the aid of your loved ones? Our niece took a sharp turn around a corner on her scooter, skidded and fell. It was two strangers who helped her up, lifted the scooter and saw her off safely.

First impressions aren't meant to benefit only us, they are necessary for our social fabric too. Just as a sword begets a sword, and what goes around comes around, empathy, politeness, and etiquette, beget great service and a helping hand from others. A kind word to a stranger spreads the kind word around. If nothing else, research proves that it makes us happy and makes us repeat our act of kindness[4].

Now, let's look at the people who offer their services to us, the battalion of maids, drivers, delivery boys, customer care executives in banks, super markets, stores, stewards at restaurants, and more. Each of them is affected by what we disclose of ourselves and how we treat them, in short, the first impressions we create and this in turn affects the quality of service they deliver to us.

But, why do I need to create an impression on them, you might ask. I am, after all, paying their wages.

To answer this question, let's take a look at what companies do. They take the pain to display their power, efficiency, learning, growth and a hundred other things to attract the right people with the right capabilities who can help them realize their goals. The same holds true for us too. If you want to attract a certain type of people who provide great service, you need to create the first impressions that attract such people.

The way you treat them, is how, in many tiny ways you retain your comfort and peace. You can't keep an untidy self and expect them to follow strict standards. Politeness to them is a necessity. Not only does it get you better service, it also strengthens our social fabric.

As we all know, the level of service we receive is not a single line, but two parallel bands within which the service level varies. Rudeness only makes the service slower and more complicated. If we want the best of service, we need to show interest and politeness. Our rudeness merely makes us look uncaring without getting us anywhere.

Anyone who has entered a car or a jewellery showroom knows best. The way you conduct yourself is how the executive perceives you. It's a rare executive who knows you for what you know is your true worth.

7. Public Lives

Some of you live public lives with a large or small audience. These lives carry blind spots since you don't have the benefit of visual and verbal cues of the strangers judging you, cues that can help you make a quick change in tone, attitude or body language. Nor do you have the comfort of having just a stranger or two to impress at a given moment. The public may number in the thousands or millions.

When your words are out in print or on the web, or when you are beamed through the television for the world to see, you are going in blind. There's no way you can gauge the response until long after the event. When it comes to the internet, once you have posted a comment up there, things are not in your control, they are up for surfing practically forever with hundreds if not thousands and millions potentially sharing your comments, posts or videos.

The spread is unimaginably wide and the number of first impressions you make is phenomenally high and there's little you can do to retract.

What do first impressions mean when that is the case? What do I do when the audience is not a single, homogenous lot? How can I cater to everyone, you might ask?
The answer is not to cater to everyone on the planet or every viewer in front of the screen. Your job is to focus on the audience that matters to you and meet their expectations. Ask yourself, who your target audience is. Do you have broad appeal? Or do you have a select audience, very niche, very choosy?

Compare the fan following of Amitabh Bachchan to that of Naseeruddin Shah. Apart from the fact that there is a huge difference in popularity, the audience which is broad based in the case of the former, shrinks to the loyal followers for a deep set of reasons in the case of the latter. Knowing your audience helps you reach out to them appropriately and create the right first impressions with the growing tribe.

Think of it, even our politicians go deep inside to know their vote bank and fine-tune their words accordingly. So it is with television programmes, movies and music. Know your audience, create that positive first impression and sustain it.

I could go all out and do a great amount of promotion and publicity. Isn't that what it takes to reach my audience?
Powerful positive first impressions aren't about extravagant marketing and hype. Many times, the most subdued and focused marketing is the right thing to do to reach your audience. By doing that, you are connecting with your tribe. Many actors and musicians are in the news for all the wrong reasons. After a certain point, there is no turning back and they move backstage in

people's minds never to regain their lost glory. They had never formed the connection in the first place.

But, why should I connect with the tribe, you might ask?

In your public lives, it is your tribe that creates your public life. Why do politicians wear the same starched white gear? They do it so that people immediately recognize that they belong to the tribe of politicians and to leave nothing in doubt about that particular first impression. Little needs to be said about their need to create the right first impressions. That's just what they are doing. Giving the tribe the chance to recognize you and to connect with you is a necessary part of your public life just as much as it is with your other lives.

The question that arises now is how should you balance these multiple lives?

We've known people who have gone all out to reach out to people, made themselves accessible and have been the center of conversations at work. But, once they reach home, they retire to their solitude where they permit no intrusion into their privacy.

There are multiple aspects to you. Doing what is needed in one life and doing what you really want to do in another is perfectly alright. After all, we live in a society with predefined norms and culture, and we have our goals and objectives to meet within these norms.

Within these multiple lives, it isn't just about choosing the most important life for you. It is about realizing that each is a part of you, big or small and to follow the rules in a way that enhances each of your lives to the extent necessary. Often, we have the tendency to prepare ourselves well in one life and leave the other lives to the wind. But, this should be a well thought out choice, rather than just a preference that takes precedence. The latter is the easy way out while the former can take you places.

It is because we are blessed with all these different lives that we can function effectively through our difficult times and our good times. One balances the other.

Now that you've come to know your lives, you know which is most important and which is not. The question arises, what can you do to create a powerful, positive first impression?

There's an art and a science to it. That's where we shall take you in Chapter 3.

REFERENCES

1 http://www.livescience.com/3468-love-sight-genetic.html

2 Archives of Sexual Behavior - http://www.dailymail.co.uk/sciencetech/article-1164600/The-look-love-Only-manage-glance-lasts-longer-8-2-seconds.html

3 http://timesofindia.indiatimes.com/city/ahmedabad/Love-at-50-Never-too-old-for-a-live-in/articleshow/10812180.cms

4 http://greatergood.berkeley.edu/article/item/kindness_makes_you_happy_and_happiness_makes_you_kind/

SO FAR

- You live many lives, but at the centre is your inner life which impacts your outer lives — the personal, social, business, virtual, transient and public lives.
- What you know of yourself, what you don't know, and what you could be, comprise your inner life.
- Knowing yourself, knowing your potential and believing in your potential, is the first step to creating powerful, positive first impressions.
- First impressions differ within different lives.
- Prioritize your lives based on what they mean to you.
- Understand the occasion, learn from observation and by asking others. This will help you know the rules for each life. Create positive first impressions accordingly.

Chapter 3

The Art and Science of First Impressions

The greatest scientists are always artists as well.

— Albert Einstein

"First impressions are just chaos." It was Nilima again, our friend from Chapter 1 who had found it difficult to believe that first impressions take place in the first few seconds of a meeting.

"Why would you say that?" I prompted her.

"It's chance, Rakesh," she said. "Chance plays the biggest role. Look at the evidence. First, people don't realize they have formed a first impression. Second, when I ask them for the logic behind the impression, they can't seem to explain it."

It was easy to understand why she felt that way. After all, isn't any logical, intelligent person supposed to collect, sift and assess all the important cues before coming to a conclusion?

"In place of the list of reasons, they come up with what they called gut feeling," she continued, "Which is a controversial topic at best when it comes to decision-making."

"A gut feeling may look mysterious, yet it's anything but illogical," I countered, stepping into the conversation. "What they called gut feeling is your brain taking note of the visual and verbal cues and coming to a rapid decision. It makes those quick decisions based on emotions, reward and fear," I said.

"But if there is intelligence to it, why can't they say it aloud? Why don't they know it themselves?"

"Well, because when people try to look for the reasons, they are not asking the part of brain that makes rapid instinctive decisions. Instead, they are asking the analytical part of it which is different and has little to do with these decisions. They are asking the wrong part of the brain."

It is, as renowned psychologist Gerd Gigerenzer has titled his book, *Gut Feelings: The Intelligence of the Unconscious.* According to him, reflection and reason are overrated. In fact, thinking about the judgments can affect your accuracy, according to psychologist Nalini Ambady who does pioneering work in the area of first impressions[1]. What scientists agree is that when asked to give the reasons for their impressions, people begin to second-guess themselves and get things wrong. When asked to think before making a decision, the judgments are not as good as when they did it without conscious effort.

Hence, people find it difficult to come to terms with the fact that first impressions happen in a few seconds and the longer they take to give the reasons, the more muddled they look, not to say with little end result.

It is little wonder then that first impressions look like chaos at work. But there is a method to this madness. Underlying every chaos is a theory that shows the order that is at work.

What is chaos theory?

Although the term chaos theory comes from the apparent disorder in systems, there is an underlying order to the random data. Pioneered by mathematician and meteorologist Edward Lorenz, it is the work of chaos theory to find this order. More importantly, that a small change in the initial conditions can drastically change the long-term behaviour of the system[2].

When applied to first impressions, although the impressions may seem random at first glance, there is an underlying order behind these rapid impressions. There is a set of initial conditions which when you change or manage, can drastically change your long-term behaviour, impact others positively and hence create powerful, positive first impressions.

So what are these initial conditions? How do they affect the system? Is there after all a method, a set of initial conditions that help you make positive and powerful first impressions?

Yes, there is a method to it. It is the art and science of creating positive and powerful first impressions.

Science is about rules and patterns that explain things. Art is about how you view a particular thing and how you go about projecting it, whether it is on paper, canvas or in the case of first impressions, your persona. So, by its very nature, art makes things different for each person and possibly for each view. A rule of science is a rule whether you read it or your colleague does. But, with art, there can be as many different impressions as the number of people viewing it.

Science without art is generic. Art without science is too random to be consistently successful. The most effective learning is when you combine the science and art behind things.

When our niece was learning to play the guitar, her mother asked the teacher how she was performing. The teacher said, "Well, if you ask me, 'Is she working hard? Is she diligent?' I would say yes. She remembers her notes. She practices at home, I can see that. But her music doesn't come to life. She isn't showing a feel for it. She doesn't know when to hold a note, when to let it go quick and let the next note slip in."

The trouble was that our niece simply played the notes by the rule, almost blindly. She had internalized the notes, not the song. Similarly, knowing the science is just half the learning. Success lies in internalizing the notes and the song, in case of first impressions, the science and the art.

What is the science of first impressions? How does it create positive first impressions?

According to one of the definitions in the Merriam-Webster dictionary, *science is a knowledge or a system of knowledge, covering general truths or the operation of general laws especially as obtained and tested through the scientific method.*

Our culture lays down the values and laws by which we live. Knowing these helps us make a conscious effort which in turn helps us maximize our lives successfully. Such an effort turns a random process into a conscious process that we can manage.

The science of first impressions provides the tools that cover these values and laws. These are the four elements of first impressions by which we project our image. When applied consciously, they help us create powerful positive first impressions, bringing greater meaning and comfort while allowing us to live to our full potential.

Elements of First Impressions

What are the four elements that can help you create positive first impressions? What are they based on?

The four elements of first impressions include clothing, grooming, body language including etiquette. They are non-verbal. To this we add vocal communication. When used judiciously, they help you project the appropriate image and thereby create powerful positive first impressions. Since first impressions are formed during the first few seconds of meeting the stranger, they are formed on the basis of non-verbal or visual communication. Vocal communication reinforces the image you project.

So, why do the elements of first impressions tend more towards the visual than vocal? After all, from everything we are told in our childhood, it is clarity of thinking, logic and vocal expression that convinces people that we are good at what we do.

In our childhood, it is the shiniest, most colourful toy that grabs our attention. As we grow older and wiser, the colours may grow less bright or shiny, but we continue to turn to visual cues to form our perception of a person. 'A picture is worth a thousand words.' So it is with you. The visual cues you present to the stranger by and large determine the first impression you create. Whether it is food and other super market products, electronics or a multitude of other products and services, it is by the packaging that we decide whether to add it to our basket or leave it on the shelf.

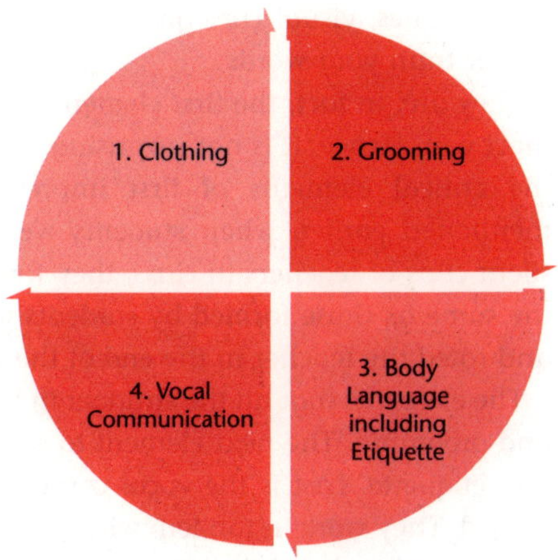

Four Elements – Science of First Impressions

Truth is, first impressions have their basis in visual cues. Take for instance Nanda interviewing candidates for a sales profile. Even as the candidate walked past the cabin's glass panels and entered the cabin, she had taken note of his clothing, demeanour, the way he opened the door, his body language, including his handshake, all this in the seconds preceding the moment when he said, "Good Morning". All are visual cues with the vocal cues coming at the very end.

In the several examples that ex-FBI agent Joe Navarro gives in his book, *What Everybody is Saying: An Ex-FBI Agent's Guide to Speed Reading People,* it is all about watching people for the visual cues they display even as they speak. This method gave him critical insights into the person's mind, particularly when the visual cues and the words were contradictory. Even when people put on a mask or speak lies, visual cues give them away. Your visual cues speak louder than your words.

They are, in fact, the first elements that strangers see when they meet you. Hence, it is not surprising that visual cues form three of the critical elements of first impressions. In related research mentioned earlier, when students were asked to rate 10-second silent clips of teachers in class, they formed impressions that were the same as those formed by students who actually took the class and rated the teacher at the end of the course.

The elements that hit the stranger in front of you first are clothing and grooming. The next element to seep in is your body language and etiquette. Last is the vocal communication by which you are judged. They work in tandem when creating first impressions. They are interrelated. While we may examine each separately, each affects the other. Each relates to the whole impression.

You might say, I have learned the postures I need to hold, how to give a firm handshake and to smile to show my readiness to answer questions. I dress well. I am good with opening conversations. I have a good start.

Take the example of Suketu whose house was under construction. He did not choose the artisans individually — the plumber, the painter, the electrician, the mason, the furnishing and fabric person, the carpenter, the person laying the tiles, the person selling the artifacts and paintings, and so on.

"I felt they would not get the big picture", said Suketu. He hired an interior decorator who took into consideration all the individual elements and brought Suketu's vision for his house to life.

When creating first impressions, learning how to manage one or two elements effectively is never enough. It is quite possible that the other elements remain in conflict with the ones you manage, leading to conflict in the image you project.

The best approach is to find out who you are deep inside to assess the outer projection based on this inner you and correct the elements accordingly. At one extreme is the highly individualized approach that focuses on yourself and pays little attention to the guidelines offered by clothing, grooming, body language including etiquette and vocal communication. At the other extreme is the highly standardized approach that makes you look like a clone of the others within the domain. Both approaches can lead to trouble because they fail to strike a balance.

Let's take Ankit, looking for the position of a research trainee in a pharmaceutical company during campus placements. He was a well above average student at academics, but a shy and retiring one who opened up once he got over the initial nervousness.

At the mock interviews, his shy nature was obvious to all. He would walk in quick nervous steps, offer a short, soft handshake and withdraw his hand immediately. After that, he wouldn't know what to do with his hands. His clothes were expensive, but they hung loose on his frame. He would fidget through the interview. Based on the feedback, he corrected his handshake, but the other visual cues remained the same.

The campus placements began soon after. When he entered the interview room, Ankit made sure that he gave a consciously powerful handshake to each of the three interviewers. But, since the other visual cues remained the same, showing his nervousness, they sent conflicting signals to the interviewers. When they asked some increasingly complicated questions to test the contradictions, he ended up stammering out his answers, leaving behind a negative impression.

Given that Ankit was applying for the position of a research trainee at the bottom of the ladder, the interviewers were looking for knowledge, capability, hard work and trustworthiness. Ankit had each of these traits, but the conflicting signals that he sent cost him the interviewers' trust.

Let's face it, first impressions aren't about creating *inaccurate* impressions that are not true to the inner you, but of avoiding *wrong* impressions that fail to reflect the inner you accurately.

A friend once said to us, "Look, this is what I am. I am not ashamed of it. What difference can the outer things make to my life? I don't have the time for them anyway."

Owner of a small furniture business, she didn't feel the need to clothe or groom herself professionally with so many competing demands on her time.

Once, she was interviewing candidates for the position of an administrative assistant and sought our help in handling the interviews. In addition to processing the paper work and handling external job workers, the candidate would have to act as assistant for our friend's own office work too. She rejected some candidates because they didn't look right for the job.

We prompted her for the reasons after each interview. At the end of the day, I pulled up each candidate's resume and the post-it note I had attached to each resume carrying our friends' comments. "Look at the reasons why you rejected them."

One comment was, "Shoes unpolished; a run down the socks. Rest of him, neat enough, but he could be cutting corners at work where it doesn't show." Another candidate was rejected, who in our friend's words 'wasn't neat enough'. And so it went.

She was surprised.

I continued. "Can you think of the number of times you knocked on the doors of interior designers and large showrooms and didn't get beyond the threshold?"

She nodded in agreement.

"Your business is doing well, grant you that, but think of where you could be if the first impression clearly indicated your competence. You are, after all, in the business of improving interiors. Think of how much more effective you would be if you showed as much care in how you project yourself as you do with an inch of chipped wood."

That was a happy ending. Plenty of us tell ourselves we don't have the time to take better care of ourselves. But think of the lost opportunities. All it takes is some learning, a bit of preparation, a few minutes each day to avoid creating negative impressions and you are ready to take advantage of those same lost opportunities.

"I need your help." The request was from Nilima, our friend who had recently come to accept the importance of first impressions. "I have an important client meeting next week and I need you to help me dress professionally."

"Give me the whole picture," said Suman. "First, what does dressing professionally mean to you?"

"It's an important corporate client we have been negotiating with for the past six months. Finally, the Head of the Purchase Department has given us an appointment and we are making the pitch the coming week. It's a big day and I want to do all I can to get everything right."

"Before we come to that, how are you preparing for the presentation?" asked Suman.

"We have been thorough in our research," said Nilima. "We spoke to people in the industry and within the company too. We have studied the market and we understand their sales cycle. So we were able to map their production and supply cycles which we re-confirmed with the inside team we are in touch with. We now know probably as much as they do about their component requirements."

"What else do you know?" asked Suman.

"Because we know their production cycle, we even know their recruitment cycle to meet the peak load months. What we sell them are the electronic components that go into the synthesizers. So, we have already discussed details with their IT people."

"Fine, but why didn't you just take your product and make the pitch to them without going into all this detail?" asked Suman.

"That's the first thing we do, we make the product pitch," Nilima explained. "But after that, it becomes just one part of the whole selling

game. The product description won't tell them more than what any competitor could tell them. See, they have some concerns which we need to address, such as whether we can meet their quality parameters, whether we can meet their production cycles, whether the product meets their IT specifications, things like that. Knowing their recruitment cycle helps us plan our training schedule to supplement theirs. At the same time, we need to know their payment terms and what suits them without hurting them. We need to address all these in our presentation or during the discussion."

"So, what you are saying is that the product is the core ingredient. Explaining that is the first level function, which I would say is the technical requirement. But you went further and looked at their business requirement, their sales, IT, HR, Finance, in short, all the related aspects, didn't you?"

"That's right," agreed Nilima.

"Let's now come back to your dressing. You are the product, Nilima. And by dressing professionally, you are enhancing the first pitch. But there are other elements which need to complement the dress element."

Nilima was silent. Suman waited patiently for her to draw the conclusion.

Finally Nilima spoke. "Oh, now I understand what you are getting at. So what are the other things that I need to get right?"

"That was quick," Suman added with a smile. "In addition to how you dress, your grooming, your body language including your etiquette, and your vocal communication, all have to be addressed as a whole to project the right image for you."

Success in making first impressions depends on your ability to work with the four elements as a whole and to apply this whole to a razor sharp judgment of the situation.

How does one go about learning to manage these four elements and implementing them? How does one know which requires greater focus?

Like we said earlier, the three important factors that influence first impressions are you, the stranger and the situation. More importantly, none of the individual elements function independently. They are interlinked and all are linked to the inner you, your inner life.

It goes without saying that a little knowledge is your own worst enemy. In such cases, ignorance is better than implementing a few elements and letting the others remain as they are. The worst you could do is to implement, for example, just the clothing and grooming guidelines and ignore body language and etiquette.

There is a method that would teach you the art of implementing the four elements, not only to create positive first impressions, but also to make sure you don't send out conflicting signals.

Your question at this point might be, What art is there to first impressions?

Going back to the Merriam-Webster dictionary for the definition of art, one of the meanings is that it is *a skill acquired by experience, study, or observation.*

While the guidelines and the technique come from the science, skill in creating powerful positive first impressions is the art. It comes from observing you, the stranger and the situation, putting into practice consistently what the science has taught you, observing the results and learning again from it.

As we have seen with many of our students, this ability seems innate at times and at other times it has been built over time. We believe it is only a matter of bringing yourself to look at reality - both within yourself and at the outside world. You need to leave preconceived notions outside the door and eliminate old habits of thinking and acting to reach that point.

Art is about taking what science has to offer and putting it to use in differing situations. Know yourself well, read the stranger and the situation well, and you will use the science effectively.

Take a chef for example. Cooking programmes teach him the finer details of the ingredients that go into cooking. They teach him how to chop, slice and dice, mix and knead. They also teach him boiling, steaming, roasting, frying, baking and the many other standardized elements of cooking. The chef also learns how to bring the flavours out and how to get the balance right. This is the science of cooking.

While learning the science, the chef develops his own flourish. He keeps in mind the restaurant style, guest expectations, the season and its ingredients to bring the dish together. He may offer a fairly standardized dish or a completely novel way of placing the pasta or the pear on your table.

In the innumerable decisions he takes when bringing together the perfect meal, he sifts through the elements he has learned. He chooses some, tones others down, adds his own twist to some elements and brings out a tasty, balanced dish that satisfies guest expectations while carrying his signature mark. This requires knowledge as well as creativity.

Success lies first in picking the important variables relevant to you, the stranger, and the situation. Then you make your choices within the elements to meet the requirements of those variables.

"All that's fine," Rajesh exclaimed when Suman explained this to the class one day. "But when it is the same situation and the same elements, everyone at campus placements will be doing the same thing. They look the same, same buttoned suits, same polished shoes, same neat grooming. How does that help me? How do I stand out?"

If you stop at the science, you will, as Rajesh fears, look like everyone else. It is the functioning of an automaton, a robot in fact. Or a production line of individual items like Ankit's overzealous powerful handshake. It is what we call the "war of the clones".

Taking Rajesh's example, campus placements for his architecture programme were a month away. His classmates were ready for the interviews with their black or deep blue jackets, matching trousers and formal shirts. They played it safe by eliminating any hint of colour. The ties were a combination of black with grey, white or blue.

To illustrate his concern, Rajesh showed the class photograph of the seniors. He was right. They did look like clones, dressed in black and white.

The trouble with clones is that the elements are implemented in a highly standardized form. As a result, the clone doesn't stand out, nor does he create a unique positive first impression. This may even lead to the perception that they follow the crowd and limit themselves to doing just what they are told. If a clone is asked to turn a bolt, well, that's just what the hundreds of clones do to the precise degree without a millimeter of deviation.

When you follow others blindly, you are likely to find yourself right in the middle of the war of the clones. This forces you to work that much more to meet your objectives, which could be gaining the position you have interviewed for, a large project, client order and so on.

In order to avoid the war of the clones, it is important to take a careful look at the industry, the company and the position you are interviewing for. Once you understand the variables involved, you would be able to choose among aspects like the line, shape, texture, colour, and pattern to create a look that is formal, yet with your own flourish.

It is the artist in you who will let you see the same people and situations with your unique perspective. Now, the scientist in you is ready to apply the guidelines. When you use a combination of the artist and the scientist, you will end up creating unique, positive first impressions that turn out to be positive lasting impressions. They will not be a replica of all the impressions that others are creating around you.

Lisa chose to follow the others and wear western formal clothing for her campus placement interview. That's where the similarity ended. She wore a silk scarf in pale blue with a small geometric pattern in red knotted neatly in front. Although she received feedback that she should play it safe and leave out the scarf because of its colours, she chose to go ahead with it.

"The entire look represented me," she said. "I observed everyone on day one of the campus placements. They were playing it safe and in the process looked the same, even the pattern of their speech to some extent. I decided to project the real me. I followed the basic guidelines of formal colours for my clothing. But I added a scarf, wore tiny dangling silver earrings rather than stud earrings. I believe the scarf stood out for its colour, yet complemented my entire attire. It brought out the softer side of me without taking attention away from the tougher side of me."

If you apply yourself to both the science and the art of first impressions, you can create positive first impressions whether in a crowd or alone, from professional campus placements and walk-in interviews, to family and other social occasions.

REFERENCES

1 http://www.guardian.co.uk/lifeandstyle/2009/mar/07/first-impressions-snap-decisions-impulse

2 http://www.imho.com/grae/chaos/chaos.html

SO FAR

- Science and art are behind creating powerful positive first impressions.
- The science behind first impressions is made of guidelines about the four elements:
    - Clothing
    - Grooming
    - Body Language & Etiquette
    - Vocal Communication.
- Visual cues influence first impressions. These include clothing, grooming, body language and etiquette.
- Each of the elements is interlinked and reflects the inner you. You need to work with them together, not individually.
- If blindly followed, the elements can make you part of the 'war of the clones'.
- The art of first impressions helps you recognize the three factors — yourself, the stranger and the situation.
- This recognition influences the way you implement the four elements so that powerful positive first impressions are created.

Chapter 4

Clothing: Dressing to Connect

Clothes make the man. Naked people have little or no influence on society.

— Mark Twain

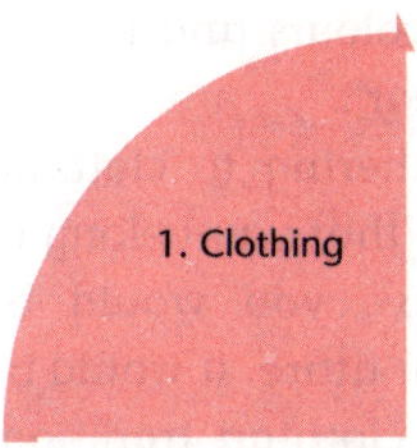

From fashion street to mall and footpath sales, clothing is a difficult-to-resist domain. There is an excitement to it that draws in even the most seemingly disinterested people.

That people derive first impressions from visual cues is known behaviour. A significant part of it is from the attire. People observe you with expectations, assumptions and preferences that make it necessary for you to have a system to manage your attire.

At our Institute, we come across a few trainees who, on the first day, ask why they need to have a system to choose their attire. In this chapter, we give you the compelling reasons behind the need for a system and what you gain by paying that attention to your clothes.

The skin is the largest organ of the human body. Covering the skin is our attire, the largest visual cue that we project to the outside world, giving us the perfect chance to make powerful positive first impressions. It is much like a second skin, reflecting our inner and outer lives, our mood, personality, values, role, status, and more. It is influenced by our audience, the occasion, and the environment, the seasons, the time of the day and to a large extent, the gender too. Clothing reflects everything, from our goals to our self-esteem.

Clothing originally evolved as a functional tool, protecting us from the environment. But, for the past many centuries, the layers of meaning that have become associated with clothing have given rise to dress codes that have become as important as its functional uses.

What are these dress codes?

To answer that question, all you have to do is look at the history of humankind. For centuries, civilizations around the world have used clothing to define and maintain strict social hierarchies.

If you had been born in Elizabethan England, you would follow The Statutes of Apparel with laws related to colours and type of clothing that define what one can own and wear[1].

Had you been born in ancient China, adhering to clothing regulations was a way for you to demonstrate that you belong to the community. Based on your social class, you would be choosing the style, fit, colour and fabric of your attire. It would be extremely important for you to respect the clothing tradition. Following the regulations indicated that order was intact and society was functioning smoothly. If for any reason you abandoned these customs, more likely than not, you would be considered a barbarian[2].

During the Japanese Heian rule, multiple layers of clothes were worn by people of stature. Had you worn inappropriate attire, it could ruin your reputation[3].

Although the rigid implementation of codes by royal decree is gone, taking its place is the silent acceptance when you meet the dress code or the resounding rejection when you don't, in business, social and personal spaces. Today, attire is how we signify age, gender, personality, values, social status, occupation, ethnic and political affiliation, even sexual display and marital status.

What do these dress codes really mean? A logical answer to this question is necessary to understand why you need to take dress codes seriously.

When the industry, club, restaurant, party or family occasion follows a dress code, what the members involved are really asking you to do is to look like you are part of their group or tribe.

In return, when you dress to suit the occasion, the people and the place, you are telling them, "I am part of your tribe."

Like attracts like. It is embedded in our brains to seek those like us and keep those dissimilar at bay. By dressing as per the dress code, you are telling them, "You are important enough for me to want to be part of your tribe." This message begets like feelings.

Families, groups, societies and companies are all different tribes. They are continuously maintaining the balance, allowing the *likes* to be part of the group and rejecting the *unlikes* outright, as in business interviews or by raising insurmountable barriers in social spaces. When our goals in life are intricately linked with a particular business, social or personal group, attaining the goal generally requires implementing their codes — the code by which the group wants us to live and by which it forms its first impressions. Clothing is a significant part of this code and corporate culture.

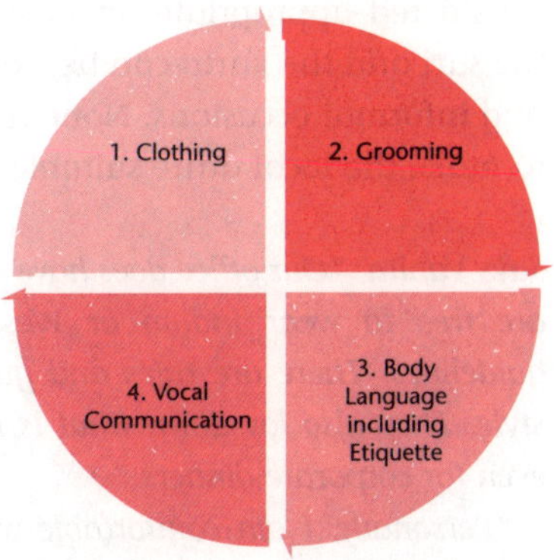

Four Elements – Science of First Impressions

There is more at stake in business scenarios than just belonging. The interviewers must assess you for something more — your knowledge, experience, competence, diligence, trustworthiness and many similar factors. Before you can become part of that company, they want to know, "Are you competent?"

If you carry the notion that your work will speak for itself and you can ignore your dress beyond being simply covered, you are mistaken. You need to dress in harmony with the company's dress code. More than that, you need to dress in harmony with the job profile so that your attire speaks accurately for you. Even before you utter a word, your attire has to say, "I am competent. Try me."

When you leave it to the verbal interaction to convey this message, it is like talking to a stranger who isn't looking at you. The interviewer is looking at your attire for an answer and you want to give her the answer verbally. Your words don't have the audience. Let your attire speak for you and it will speak louder than your words.

These are two very powerful statements in the personal, social and business contexts — 'I belong to your tribe'. and 'I am competent'. From the bottom of the corporate ladder to the top, they apply to everyone in the hierarchy. It is never absent.

According to research conducted in the USA, applicants wearing standard or custom suits were more likely to be offered a job than those in casual attire[4]. In some countries, the local dress could be considered appropriate for business wear. For instance, in India, the sari and the kurta can be worn by women to a range of formal and informal occasions. Nonetheless, there is a system and a scale to make the local attire suitable for each occasion.

Says Vanita, "Our office does have a fairly strict dress code. But then, we are free to wear Indian or Western wear, provided we follow the guidelines. There are rules and guidelines for colours, the fit and the style. They also lay down what is right for office, meetings and travel, even for corporate dinners."

"Personally, I am comfortable with a salwar-kurta. But, I choose to wear western formal wear on most days for its formal look and colours.

It isn't as easy getting the formal colours in Indian wear. But whenever I find a kurta that follows the guidelines of formal clothing, I buy it. This helps me shift between Indian and Western wear while retaining the formal look."

But, does attire really matter in today's world where we wear our *self* on our sleeve?

Attire matters because it is the tool by which we project our nature, personality, competence, self-confidence and more to the stranger. Not only is there a need to have the positive traits within us, there is a great need to display them too. In addition, clothing influences our perceptions of ourselves and hence of how we work. When Professor Adam D. Galinsky, a professor at the Kellogg School of Management at Northwestern University and his colleague, Hajo Adam, studied the effect of clothing on cognitive processes, they found that the symbolic meaning of clothes and the physical experience of wearing them influenced the psychological processes[5]. In their study, participants wearing a white lab coat, which they believed belonged to a doctor, showed a sharp rise in their ability to pay attention.

Secondly, people relate well to those who belong to their tribe. By following the dress code of the stranger, the company or the industry, you communicate the message that you belong to their tribe. In doing so, you make it easier for them to form positive first impressions.

If attire didn't matter in today's world, job interviewers would not come to quick conclusions based on how good a fit your attire is according to the job profile. Clubs would not have strict dress codes. Head waiters at high-end restaurants would not look down their noses if you sauntered in to their location in crumpled T-shirts, torn jeans and sandals. You would not wear white when mourning in a western country or black to marriages in India. Of all the social codes, none is more specific to occasion than your attire. Formal dinners would have no reason to inform you that it is a black tie dinner. Families would not take care to dress up to celebrate special occasions with the members in their intimate and personal spaces.

But, "I want to be myself," you might say. "Changing my attire to suit a person or a situation just isn't me."

The entire concept of first impressions is about flexibility. As much as there is a system to donning the right attire, the system itself offers tremendous flexibility. It offers broad guidelines and within those guidelines, there is plenty of leeway for you to create a look just for yourself with great comfort too. Look at the successful men and women around you. Pick the Fortune 500 CEOs or the most powerful women in business or in an industry. At a superficial glance, they might look like they are dressed in the same suits, skirts or saris. A closer look will tell you the truth — not one of them is dressed the same as another. They project their individual persona through their attire.

Just as attire offers you this flexibility, it also demands from you a flexibility of thought and a readiness to accept an attire if you are new to it. Before you tell yourself, I am fine the way I am, ask yourself what your priorities are — To dress the way you like? Or to reach your goal? Remember, first impressions have the single, largest positive impact on your success in your personal, social and business spaces.

"Dress codes?" said Leena. She is a social media consultant with years of experience. "They are just guidelines. Not a rule book. I am not in the police force or the defense! There's no logic to treating dress codes as uniforms. Sure, I follow the dress code, but I have my quirks. So, I wear dresses and accessories the way they suit me. All the while, I am following the dress code. Take the scarf for example. I am in love with scarves. Summer, rain or winter, I have a scarf about me. Granted, they are allowed within the dress code. Where I bring in my uniqueness is in the way I wear the scarf. I might wrap it around my head, knot it at the

back, let it hang loose on a shoulder or around my neck. There are plenty of things I can do with each piece of the attire," she laughed.

What are people judging by your attire anyway?

In a split second, people may be drawing inferences about your socio-economic status[6]. They are forming first impressions about your level of education, your profession and career track. Your attire also indicates your personality and values, your psychological disposition and hence your attractiveness to the stranger.

Dress appropriately and you can be seen as an intelligent, successful achiever. If you don't, you could easily be the tramp, a shirker or an untrustworthy person so that they are loath to allow you to step into their social, personal or intimate spaces. Based on the visual cues from your attire, they are forming their impressions and this determines how they communicate with you and the relationship they will form with you. This is called impression formation.

The question now arises, are all strangers going to judge you the same way?

No, they are not. Just as you have your uniqueness, the stranger in front you — the interviewer, principal, stranger at a party, prospective spouse — each has his or her own perspective and way of looking at people. They are influenced by who they are and what they expect from you in the situation. Depending on the situation, one takes precedence over the other.

Neena, a mid-level HR manager says, "When I interview a candidate, the job profile and what's good for the company takes precedence. I will admit there is a seeping in of how I view people in general, but the priority is the job and the company. After all, I am not paid to like a candidate. There have been candidates whom I would not like or relate to personally, but I know they are good for the profile. On the contrary, if

I am at a social gathering, my personal preferences come first. Do I like this person at all? That's the primary question. Naturally, I expect a certain behaviour on certain occasions. But I am free to think from my personal space."

Speed dating is a perfect example of the impact of first impressions. Introduced for the first time in the 1990s by Rabbi Yaacov Deyo to help Jewish singles in Los Angeles meet one another in 4 minute "dates", it has been rapidly accepted by the public[7]. Today, speed dating procedures form the basis of further research by social scientists for the wealth of psychological insights they offer into how humans form their romantic impressions within minutes.

Clear evidence came up in an experiment[8] in which researchers asked the participants to ask for dimes to make a phone call. "Well-dressed participants received more money at the airport. Poorly dressed participants received more money at the bus station." Strangers' judgments are not uniformly the same in all situations. Their perceptions and expectations in a certain situation or environment impacts the way they judge you.

As we have explained with the three factors that impact first impressions — you, the stranger, the situation — impressions differ from stranger to stranger. Fashion-conscious strangers notice the attire more than those who have little interest in fashion[9]. Since you don't know what the interviewer's preferences are likely to be, it makes enormous sense to follow the dress code for every interview.

Given these uncertain circumstances, how do you make sure that you've dressed to achieve your goal?

If that was all there was to attire, wearing neat formal attire for business occasions and casual attire for informal occasions, things would be simple. Reality is that people have different expectations at different levels of the business and social hierarchy, even family hierarchy for that matter. These expectations impact the first impressions they seek in the attire.

Perceptions related to your competence are at stake here. The interviewer is taking a split-second glance at your attire, coming to a judgment about you and extrapolating your competence, credibility and other characteristics from this judgment.

Look at yourself in the mirror before you leave home for the interview, think of the job profile and ask yourself, "Do I look like I already hold that job?"

If it is a yes, you are ready to step out for the interview. If it is not, and you can't figure out why, think of a person who already holds that position successfully. Let their appearance give you direction in making corrections to your own attire.

Years ago, when we met Khyati, she was a mid-level marketing executive in a textile company. She had learned early on to look to "those ahead" of her as she put it. When we probed deeper, "There is always someone ahead of you," she said. "At the campus, it was the seniors. It was a revelation to me. Seniors, who would usually saunter casually between classes in torn, much-worn jeans and T-shirts, were suddenly striding with a more confident step wearing suits and polished shoes at placement time on campus."

When she applied for a managerial position in a textile company, she was carrying in her mind images of executives already in that position from her old company. "That's a good rule any day," she said. "Watch your seniors in the company. But I was shifting industries from a software firm to the textile industry and I decided I had to be more cautious. I called the HR department and asked them what the marketing people were expected to wear in the company. Their advice definitely helped me tweak my attire with small, but very necessary changes."

"It pays to check the company code," she added, "or even the department's. Creative agencies by necessity have a different dress code for their creative and client servicing departments. It's quite clear that the client servicing executives have a formal dress code, but I've seen

visualizers and copy writers walk in with what I can only say is business casual attire at best. Sometimes, it's hard to call it even that," she smiled.

Does all this mean there has to be a *fit* between attire and job profile?

Rather, we call it the *fit* between attire and goals. Your attire must be based on goals — yours and the stranger's. It is about what you want to gain from the meeting while the interviewer judges you based on what she wants to gain from you.

Look at what research reveals. Applicants wearing suits were rated more appropriate for higher level positions compared to those wearing casual attire[10]. Interviewers' impressions differed for entry level positions and higher level positions. For an entry-level position, they found applicants wearing high-end clothing less attractive. For higher level positions, they found applicants in standard business suits more attractive than those in cheaper clothing.

The end result is that, people wearing casual attire came out creating impressions of lower competence. On the other hand, those wearing a suit created impressions of higher competence. Clearly, the attire is sending a signal to the interviewer about your competence. If, in these few seconds, you are waiting to speak with logic, experience and knowledge, you are too late.

Nowhere is attire more important than in customer-facing situations. From corporate uniforms in banking, retail, hospitality, travel and healthcare industries to stringent dress codes in other industries, companies expect their employees to dress for competence, trustworthiness and approachability.

According to research, three factors made customers more inclined to make a purchase based on what the sales executive in the store has said — the executive's knowledge of the product, appropriate attire for the environment and whether the executive was open and friendly with the client[11]. Leave out any one of the three factors and the client is disinclined to make the purchase.

The higher the stakes, the higher the presence of a rigidly defined dress code. If you are in financial services, high-end clothing or jewellery stores or luxury car showrooms, it is critical for you to stick closely to the dress code. The customer should want to trust you with her money. That happens only when your attire communicates confidence, capability and trustworthiness.

But if you ask the strangers, How did the attire affect your first impressions, you will get different answers, ranging from "It didn't affect one bit," to "The attire said it all for him". How then do you judge between *what they say* and *what they mean* about the impressions they have formed?

When you ask people directly, they are more likely to say that clothes didn't matter in their consideration. But according to social psychology, attitude matters. An attitude is a positive or negative evaluation of people, objects, events and others. If the attitude is explicit and socially accepted, people will be ready to express it verbally. But if their attitude is implicit, they would not express it verbally. It is the non-verbal clues like clothing, grooming and body language that you have to observe.

What about social occasions? Is there a *fit* between attire and the occasion operating here too?

Ranging from casual family gatherings, to fun lunches with friends to casual official dinners, to highly formal dinners, each of these social gatherings has a dress code of its own. What is right for a club may not be right for a pub. What is right for a marriage ceremony isn't what you'd wear for the office party. What you'd wear to a New Year celebration is different from what you take pains to clothe yourself in to a formal dinner in honour of a distinguished guest.

Your attire must *fit* with the occasion or you will stand out like a sore thumb. If you don't know, don't hesitate to ask the host. Or ask your peers if it is an official dinner. Make sure you have a few mix-

and-match items that will work well for several social occasions. Although repeating the items may not be very visible at work, it is far more noticeable at social occasions.

"What about personal occasions?" Suman and I were asked once. "I don't mind sticking to the rules in business and social attire, but I am me in my personal life. I am supposed to meet the prospective groom and my family forces me to wear a sari, which I rarely do. I am more into jeans and T-shirts or jeans and kurta at best. Am I not giving a wrong impression? What if they expect me to dress and behave like a demure, sari-wearing daughter-in-law?"

Wearing a sari when you are formally meeting a prospective spouse or his family is not an indication of the kind of person you are. By wearing a sari, you are following a long-standing tradition and in doing so, you are showing that the occasion is very important to you. That's the first impression you are trying to create, that you are willing to accommodate. At the same time, by wearing the sari and accessorizing it to your taste, you show your individuality.

The real question here is from a generation caught between the old and the new. It comes as a relief that while the older generation would like to see you holding up traditions on important occasions, they don't expect you to live by those traditions every day of your life. So we advise our students and clients that they can go ahead and follow the tradition, but make it clear in their daily life that they are a new generation with a life of their own.

Parents are often frustrated with their teenager's attire. "It's got a tear in it, many in fact," they tell us, "Things are slipping and sliding or they are too tight. There's clanking, jangling stuff and stuff too uncomfortable to sit down in. Is there any way we can get them to listen to us?"

To no other group is fitting into the tribe more of a problem than for teens. To set themselves apart from their parents' generation, they adhere to fashion that is all their own. In their highly casual Western style dressing, teens have a strict code of attire and can be part of the tribe or an outcast simply on its basis. Our advice to parents is to have overall guidelines. Rather than be rigid, these guidelines should offer flexibility to teens and parents in deciding what is acceptable for a particular occasion.

A student whom Nita recalled from her under-graduate engineering years, Anshuk was a study in polish and grooming, while all the other students were in torn jeans, chappals and in T-shirts that never saw an iron. Anshuk wore neatly pressed trousers and shirt with a leather belt each day. The only concession he would make was to wear Penny Loafers.

"To tell you the truth," said Nita, "There wasn't much wrong with him, but he appeared so out of place. He was doing the wrong thing at the wrong time. Today, when all of us are working, if he dressed the way he had done then, which I am sure he is, he wouldn't stand out a bit. But, back then, during our under graduate years, it was asking for trouble.

Is attire important in the personal space, for men or women at home?

Whether you are a man or a woman back home from the office, a home maker, a new mother who is taking a break or a newly-wed in a new country finding your feet before you take the work plunge, it is important to take care of your attire. From personal to social occasions, taking care of your attire gives you that feeling of confidence and makes others comfortable in your presence. Attire is also the means by which you show that you care.

Open the door in mussed hair, crumpled slacks or stained kurtas and the impression you create on the spouse, child or impromptu guest is that you are not entirely neat. You are giving them a chance to extrapolate based on this one impression about your competence, care and warmth. What applies to the social and business space applies to the personal space too.

On the other hand, when you are groomed well and are dressed for the occasion, whether it is for a personal, social or business occasion, you exude ability, competence and authority. People observe you and come to a conclusion regarding your attributes based on these observations.

Having come so far, we need to share a word about fashion and attire, because many mistake fashion trends for good, appropriate clothing.

No discussion about attire can be complete without referring to fashion. While fashion is about novelty and creativity, appropriate attire is about you, the stranger and the situation. If fashion meets the requirements of the variables involved in these three factors, it is right for you. If it doesn't, it is wrong for you at that point in time, given that particular situation with that stranger. Proper attire cannot be driven completely by fashion. But, there is a definite overlap between fashion and the appropriate attire.

According to research, when male and female college students evaluated a female student, their impressions were that she was more sociable when she wore clothing that was in fashion than when she wore attire that was out of fashion[12].

Keep track of the current trends, but dress to your goals. That is our advice to all who make a serious effort to create powerful positive first impressions through their attire.

In conclusion, attire is a powerful weapon. Nowhere is the power it holds more evident than in the voice it raises in dissent. Social, economic and political movements have used attire to send a clear and strong message of dissent to authorities.

Just as attire is a form of belonging to a tribe, it is also a form of showing dissent. By burning the clothes, we send the clear, unadulterated message, "We do not belong to your tribe."

The Indian Swadeshi movement where British clothing was burned sent an economic and political message. The economic strategy was the boycott of British products and the revival of domestic products, thereby improving domestic economic conditions. The political objective was the removal of the British Empire from power.

In a milder form, by turning up in the wrong attire, you are telling the stranger in front that you couldn't care less about being there. You force the interviewer to conclude that you don't care about the job or the company. You leave the host, who has gone to great trouble to organize a successful party, with the impression that coming to the party was the least important of your priorities. At home, you leave the spouse to wonder if life with him or her is no longer important to you. With that, you set the ground for their reaction.

An excessively casual dress promoted by the American business casual trend sends a negative message. Sloppy and deconstructed dresses do not project the image of ability and competence. On the contrary, the negative message that they send take control of the situation away from your hands.

Forget everything else for a moment. When you are appropriately attired, you give yourself a powerful message of confidence which reflects in the way you work, your body language and how you respond to the world.

REFERENCES

1 http://www.elizabethanenglandlife.com/clothing-in-elizabethan-england.html

2 http://www.kwintessential.co.uk/articles/china/ancient-china-clothing/2372

3 http://www.facts-about-japan.com/ancient-japan.html

4 Understanding the Impact of Applicant Attire on Interviewer Perceptions, by Cassandra Janelle Barger

5 Journal of Experimental Social Psychology - http://vestexprotects.com/system/pdfs/34/original/does_what_you_wear_affect_how_you_act_2012.pdf

6 Rosenfeld & Plax, 1977

7 http://faculty.wcas.northwestern.edu/eli-finkel/documents/33_FinkelEastwick2008_CDir.pdf

8 The Effects of Attire, Location, and Sex on Aiding Behavior - Hensley (1981), Sourced from Effects of Graduate Teaching Assistant Attire on Student Learning , Misbehaviors, and Ratings of Instruction, by David K.Roach

9 Understanding the Impact of Applicant Attire on Interviewer Perceptions - Cassandra Janelle Barger

10 Understanding the Impact of Applicant Attire on Interviewer Perceptions – Cassandra Janelle Barger

11 Research by Bergeren, Fallu and Roy (2008) sourced from Understanding the Impact of Applicant Attire on Interviewer Perceptions - Cassandra Janelle Barger

12 Clothing Style Differences: Their Effect on the Impression of Sociability - Johnson, Nagasawa, and Peters (1977) Sourced from Effects of Graduate Teaching Assistant Attire on Student Learning , Misbehaviors, and Ratings of Instruction, by David K.Roach

SO FAR

- Success at creating positive first impressions depends on the ability to manage the four elements as a whole — clothing, grooming, body language including etiquette and vocal communication.
- Your attire is a powerful visual cue and plays a strong role in creating positive first impressions.
- Clothing communicates two powerful positive messages — 'I belong to your tribe', and 'I am competent'.
- Your attire speaks louder than your words. Successful people project their appropriate, authentic and unique persona through their clothing.
- By your clothing, people draw inferences regarding your socio-economic status, level of education, profession and career track.
- They also draw inferences about your personality, psychological disposition and your attractiveness.
- Visual cues from the attire influence how strangers communicate with you and the relationship they will form with you.
- Strangers judge you based on who they are and what they expect from you in the situation. Pay attention to both.
- There must be harmony between your attire and
    - your goal
    - the occasion
    - the stranger's expectations
- Give teens the freedom to make their choice regarding their clothing within certain boundaries.
- Keep track of the current trends, but dress to achieve your goals.

Chapter 5

Grooming – The Power of the Perfect Look

I can't change the direction of the wind, but I can adjust my sails to always reach my destination.

— Jimmy Dean

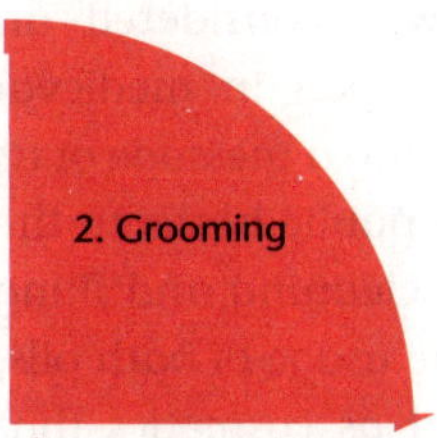

Grooming is more than brushing the teeth, bathing, shaving and combing the hair. It is a form of communication and has its share of influence in creating positive first impressions. Consider its ancient history and the extent to which our ancestors went to ensure what they considered good grooming.

What is similar between the early hominids, also known as great apes, and humans is that grooming was a language through which the species communicated important things. Those early hominids, according to British anthropologist, Robin Dunbar's premise[1], understood the importance of relationships and for lack of language, communicated through mutual grooming behaviour. This was a way to create and maintain friendships, determine the hierarchy within the tribe and make the social relationships known to others.

With humans, the tribes got too big to maintain lengthy grooming sessions to signal social relationships and language evolved. Direct speech is a more concise way of communicating relationships.

Grooming in the current sense, with its importance going beyond cleanliness and hygiene, had its beginnings thousands of centuries ago when Neanderthal men filed their teeth, in addition to painting and tattooing their faces and bodies way back in 100,000 B.C[2]. If you thought aversion to body hair is a fairly modern phenomenon, well, modern Neanderthals also pulled hair from the head and body to alter their appearance. They even invented tweezers, using shells. Around 30,000 BC, men started using flint razors to shave.

As humankind evolved and complex societies emerged, humans indulged in lengthy rituals of grooming and beauty care. The higher up the social hierarchy you were, in all probability, the longer the time you spent in grooming yourself.

Barring a few centuries when bathing was considered an invitation to illness and hence looked down upon in medieval Europe, grooming took on a personality, conveying a message of its own. It encompassed a range of activity from public baths to the eventual usage of soap, from hair removal to cleaning and filing teeth, from fresh breath by chewing herbs to the usage of bath oils, perfumes, powders and hair perfumes as well as cosmetics that include make-up, eye paint and lipsticks.

What is the relevance of grooming in the current world?

Picture the scenario — you have entered the interview, hair and tie askew, shoes scuffed, your suit could do with a press. Unfortunately for you, the interview is at the end of the day and there is just a hint of staleness about you, not to speak of the oily facial skin you had tried to wipe clean.

You are waiting for the interview to begin to convince the

interviewers how good you are, and how right you are for the company.

Stop right there for a second.

As you sit there expectantly, the interviewer has already formed her first impression of you. *"A rookie who can't cut the grade."* Or *"A tough cookie off the street who is not qualified for the job or the company."*

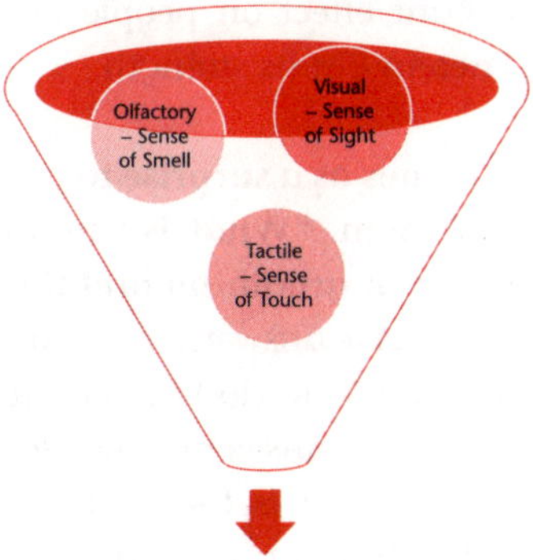

Senses of Grooming

You have, in a moment, projected yourself as a person who cannot take care of himself. To the interviewer, this is a red flag and they have extrapolated your appearance to aspects of the job.

Out of 500 HR professionals in a Gillette sponsored survey[3], 84 per cent agreed that well-groomed employees climb the corporate ladder faster than those who are not well-groomed. If this is true for employees whose work and diligence is known to bosses, peers, team members and the HR department, it is evident that you don't stand a chance as you sit ill-groomed for the interview.

If you are thinking of impressing your interviewers with your competence and capability yet pay little attention to grooming, you've lost the immense value that this asset could deliver for you.

Some 90 per cent of these HR professionals said that in interviews, they placed the greatest importance on the candidate being well-groomed, even more than a firm handshake. Remember, it is HR professionals who screen you before you meet the department heads who in fact take an in-depth look at your experience and knowledge. If your grooming is neglected, you have fallen at the first hurdle.

Again, these HR professionals said that if the candidate showed up unkempt and slovenly for interviews, it gave them the impression that they don't want the job[4]. Grooming has that instant effect on people and it works on more senses than one. Therein lies its strength.

It comes as a surprise to our trainee image consultants when we ask them, "What is the most important differentiating factor between grooming and the other elements?"

We receive answers, ranging from 'it is about the person' to 'neatness as opposed to clothing or manners' to 'health and hygiene'.

The last answer comes closest to the truth. It is our senses.

Grooming is the element that reaches out to two, even three senses that have a noticeable effect on the first impressions created. Its impact is more complex and far stronger than is usually understood.

Much about first impressions is related to visual cues — the *sense of sight*. Grooming does a close follow-up to your attire, forming a critical visual cue. You may have the right clothes on, but without appropriate grooming, the entire visual cue goes wrong. Taking care of your skin, face, hair, and nails are important aspects that create a positive first impression.

The interesting fact about grooming is the olfactory cues — the *sense of smell* — it provides. For thousands of centuries, it has been a key sense used in intimate, personal and social spaces, making grooming a subtle, yet powerful medium. Body odour can put people off from an otherwise likeable persona. Today, body odour is prevented not just with a daily wash but with the use of deodorants in addition to shampoos and mouth fresheners.

The third sense that grooming impacts is the *sense of touch* — the tactile cue — relevant primarily to intimate and personal spaces. But, it also has its relevance in business and social spaces. A dry, smooth palm is as necessary as a firm handshake in creating positive first impressions. When it comes to intimate and personal spaces, the texture of skin and hair plays an important role in bringing individuals closer and strengthening the bond between them. This includes the softness and freshness of the skin and hair which is possible by caring for them.

Reaching out to these three senses makes grooming a well-rounded element, the absence of which means that you have lost a strong ally in creating powerful positive first impressions.

Grooming is like the layers you wrap yourself up in winter. It is common knowledge that layers of covers are warmer than a single thick blanket. Similarly, the layered cues of senses produce a multiplier effect in comparison to working with a single sense.

So, what is the message conveyed through grooming?

Grooming shifted centuries ago from the message of health and hygiene to the realm of strengthening business, social and personal relationships. Today, it is used to convey subtle communication related to your socio-economic status, interest in a person, family, gathering or company, while projecting your persona.

The basic message you convey is, "Look, I am capable of taking care of myself." By extension, you imply, "I can take responsibility for your work, money and such things under consideration and with appropriate attention to detail."

The advanced message you convey is of ease and quiet confidence. Strangers around you need just that one look to decide whether they can place confidence in you.

Of the three senses that grooming encompasses, it is the visual and olfactory senses that are important in your personal, social and public lives. Hence, we shall deal with these two. The sense of touch is a medium largely for intimate spaces, except when it comes to a handshake, which we shall deal with in the section on body language and etiquette.

Grooming is best understood when we separate it into the basic and advanced levels.

Levels of Grooming

BASIC LEVEL

The basic level is about hygiene, the physical care of your body. That is the foundation grooming rests on.

Visual Cues

The visual cues influencing the sense of sight depend on hygiene with specific care for skin, nails, teeth and hair — the visual cues you display at first glance. It involves daily brushing of teeth, bathing, taking care of your body, your skin, nails and hair across different seasons, particularly the face. It involves managing a range of skin-related issues from dandruff to acne to oily or dry skin.

Olfactory Cues

Basic olfactory cues influencing the sense of smell rely on preventing malodor like bad breath, body odour and strong odour from the hair, clothing and footwear. Bad breath is a silent hurdle that prevents people from stepping closer within your social, personal and intimate spaces. Preventing odours of any kind, at any time of the day or season of the year involves taking care of your body and clothes, including your socks and shoes which can otherwise announce your arrival with the equivalent of an olfactory bang.

Levels of Grooming

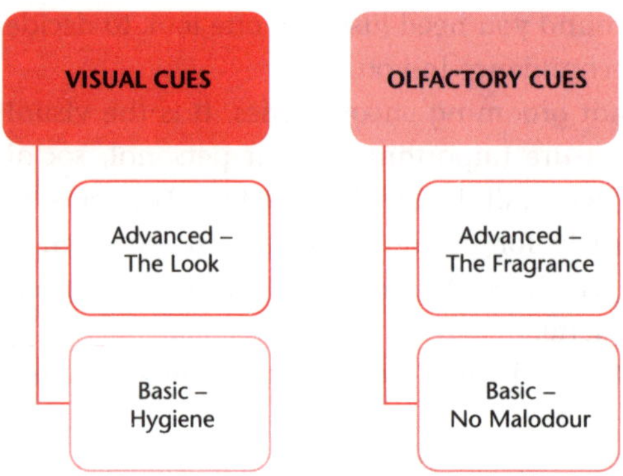

At risk of repeating ourselves, we advise a daily bath, twice or more in hot climates, whenever you leave for an important occasion, personal, social or business. In addition, from antiperspirants and deodorants to perfumed soaps, it's a matter of a few minutes each day to make sure that you smell as clean as you look.

Emitting the perfect olfactory cue too is not just about taking care of the exterior, but also about eating the right food, keeping your breath fresh and keeping yourself calm — the internal factors of odour.

Raw garlic or onion, alcohol and other such substances leave traces of bad breath and even manifest in the form of body odour. Consumption of cigarettes leaves you with a stale nicotine breath which is a definite put-off to most people. This stands universal across business, social, personal and more importantly, your intimate spaces.

Further, your emotions are transmitted through your odour. "I could smell his fear a mile away," though an exaggeration is a reality. Being at peace, although not simple, is the remedy.

The closer the stranger stands to you, the greater the impact of olfactory cues in creating first impressions. Considering that most business, all social, personal and intimate interactions involve physical proximity, olfactory cues are more powerful than they are usually credited with.

We sat late in our office one evening to interview candidates for a senior administrative position. The person would be responsible for organizing and running the image consulting classes smoothly and handling the myriad things that require coordination. It also meant interacting with trainee consultants and visiting faculty.

One candidate who seemed the right fit was polite and neat in attire and had the experience, yet something wasn't right about him. As we sat across the table, I focused on him to find the source of my discomfort even as I asked the routine questions.

And then I knew. A faint odour emanated from him. At the end of a long day, it's difficult not to leave a whiff of it. But, even if I set aside the fact that we trained people in image management and first impressions, this was an interview. Had he been serious about the job and taken care to understand its requirements, he would come meeting all expectations. That includes taking care of body odour.

ADVANCED LEVEL

Things get exciting at the advanced level. It can take you a step or many steps above the basic level, based on your preference. It is here that you play to the senses, your own and the stranger's. Here is where you project your own persona. At the same time, it is a powerful means of drawing in the strangers around you.

Visual Cues

Visual cues influencing the sense of sight involve minimizing facial hair for both men and women through plucking, tweezing, waxing, shaving, bleaching and for men a compulsory morning shave too. While some cultures accept facial hair like moustache and beard in men, the safer bet is to have a clean shaven face, certainly in customer-facing professions.

It also includes covering up visible body hair by buttoning the shirt right up to the neck in formal or even business casual occasions. The only time it is okay to display body hair is in your intimate or personal space. These are the accepted customs and hence expected of you today.

Although neatly combed hair is a basic visual cue for most men and women today, the hair is a way to reflect personality and individuality. This is evident from the fact that no two hair styles look alike. The stylist may have done the exact same thing for two people, but the shape of their face and head, the way they carry the hairdo, and the tiny changes they make in combing make all the difference.

Real leverage comes in the form of make-up for women adding much-needed contrast — a possible foundation or powder, eye shadow, liner and mascara and a touch of lipstick. There are many shades to choose from. Each woman, based on the occasion, season and time of the day, but most importantly, her own persona, chooses the cosmetics that retain her individuality while projecting an image that attracts positive first impressions.

While highlighting your most attractive features, you can go from the natural look to a perfectly coiffed look with not a hair out of place. You can highlight selected attributes, depending on your company, peers, customers, friends or family in business, social or personal gatherings. The only rule to follow is, never let your grooming be a source of distraction in business environments.

Olfactory Cues

The olfactory cues involve carrying a subtle fragrance wherever you go. It encompasses your body and where you can influence it, your surroundings too.

Nothing is more personal than the perfume or deodorant one chooses. While deodorants are essential and are available in a range of fragrances, it is perfumes that offer the full range to meet the needs of intimate, personal and social spaces. Whether you choose to carry a characteristic fragrance or to explore and use the right one for each occasion, it is entirely up to you. But make sure it is a mild, natural fragrance. Many people are allergic to strong fragrances.

While many focus on body fragrance, they forget the hair. What is fragrance in one part of the world may be viewed as pungent in another region. The safest practice is to keep the fragrance light. Some people are allergic to strong smells, hence, the essential rule is never to be overpowering, just a gentle trace of fragrance.

If the meeting is at your home or business space, fragrance in the room is another often forgotten olfactory cue that can be taken advantage of.

The smell must complement the surroundings. If you end up using a light floral fragrance in the meeting room, it is likely to be out of place because of the soft, feminine overtones it carries. Coffee and tea are the accepted norm at work places. So, during business occasions, it can be the smell of fresh coffee.

For social occasions, the fragrance of fresh flowers, from lilac to lavender to jasmine and many others are ideal. They lighten the mood and relax the guests.

Food being a favourite ingredient at personal gatherings, the aroma of a favourite dish or fresh baked cake, bread or brownies can be appealing. There are times when one space overlaps another, for example, when you have a business dinner. On such occasions, it is time to choose the most appropriate fragrance.

Take care that with each of these fragrances you have guest sensitivity in mind. Some find certain flower fragrances overpowering, like jasmine. A vegetarian guest may not find the smell of non-vegetarian dishes appealing. Avoid artificial fragrances as they can leave a strong after odour that many find overpowering or are allergic to.

How would you know which visual or olfactory cue is the requisite one for an occasion?

Visual cues, with very few exceptions, are the first cues that strangers take in. But, as the person moves closer to you in physical space, it is the olfactory sense that takes precedence. The stranger's sense of sight may go further than their sense of smell, but smell leaves a stronger imprint than sight for some people.

Daniel had met Nikita at a business conference. "I was having an interesting conversation when a lady introduced herself to our group. I had seen her approach us from a distance with just passing interest.

Close up, she looked neat as a pin in trouser and kurta, but her hair had a bubbly life of its own, that's the best I can describe it, stopping her appearance from being too sharp and severe. The genuine smile that lit up her eyes exuded an appealing warmth.

She had this faint fragrance about her of jasmine, and to me jasmine meant my aunt's home back in my childhood and her tall bed which I'd climb onto with difficulty. She would be leaning against it ready with stories for us after the day's work. She had been my uncle's wife and had this aura of serenity about her.

I couldn't help watching Nikita closer. Although she had the neat scrubbed look from afar, on closer look I found that she had a trace of make-up. At the moment, she was the perfect combination of natural and glamour — just divine."

REFERENCES

1 http://www.msnbc.msn.com/id/20642550/ns/technology_and_science-innovation/t/how-social-can-we-get/#.TtuWsmNCq0s - Also http://www.hup.harvard.edu/catalog.php?isbn=9780674363366

2 http://www.guyspy.com/history-mens-grooming

3 http://brettchatz.blogspot.com/2009/09/gillette-career-advantage.html

4 http://blogs.cio.com/meridith_levinson/extreme_makeover_it_job_seekers_may_need_appearance_upgrade

SO FAR

- Grooming reaches out to three senses, producing a multiplier effect in creating positive first impressions:
  - Visual — Sense of Sight
  - Olfactory — Sense of Smell
  - Tactile — Sense of Touch
- Grooming conveys the message, 'I am capable of taking care of things with attention to detail'.
- Grooming can be understood through the basic and advanced levels of senses.
- The basic level is about maintaining hygiene (visual) and preventing malodour (olfactory).
- The advanced level works with the look (visual) and fragrance (olfactory)
- Grooming involves taking care of the body, skin, face, nails, hair and teeth.
- It also involves controlling body odour, odour from clothes and footwear, strong odour from hair and bad breath.
- Sense of sight may go farther than the sense of smell, but smell leaves a stronger imprint than sight for some.

Chapter 6

Body Language & Etiquette – Managing How Your Body Talks

What you do speaks so loud that I cannot hear what you say.

— Ralph Waldo Emerson

3. Body Language including Etiquette

What is your first impression of the stranger at the party with a warm smile and making eye contact with you as you speak? Or of the candidate who slouches on the other side of the interview table, leaning away? Or the teen who drums his leg as you admonish him for what he's done?

All these and more reflect the person's emotions and state of mind as expressed through his body language.

Rashmi stood talking to the man she had met moments ago at her friend's birthday party. She was an interior designer and he, a copy writer. The conversation had started promisingly enough, but it took all of two minutes for Rashmi to start feeling uncomfortable and she found herself demonstrating the classic defensive postures. She stiffened then leaned backward, folding her arms across her body. The discomfort continued because the man stood too close for comfort, less than a foot away from her. She took a step backward. It didn't help, because he had taken a step forward to compensate. At one point, a person passing behind him must have brushed against his back because his whole body swung forward and she instinctively lifted one hand as if warding him off. She moved backward again and he, another step forward. This awkward dance continued until she found herself backed against a potted plant.

By now, her answers were polite, she was no longer initiating a new topic. A stiff smile appeared that didn't reach her eyes and her eyes darted about. The moment another member joined them, she slipped away and kept her distance from the man for the rest of the evening.

Many things were happening here.

- The man had stood too close for comfort.
- Rashmi's posture stiffened, she leaned back and folded her arms.
- She stepped backward.
- She put her hand up to ward him off.
- Her smile no longer reached her eyes.
- Her eyes darted instinctively looking for a means to escape.
- She no longer initiated a new topic in the conversation.

When asked, here is what Rashmi had to say, "I didn't expect a stranger to crowd me. He had walked into my personal space. It was as if he had pushed through into my home and made himself comfortable on the couch."

Looked at as a group, it is a story of one person's overtures and his blindness to the other's negative response. The important thing about body language is not just to remain open and friendly, but also to be receptive to the message the other person conveys. By remaining completely indifferent to her responses, the man had put her off further, not allowing a chance for a mutually interesting conversation or a relationship to develop.

What message do we convey through our body language?

Focusing on the positive messages that you can convey through body language, they can range from 'I am open to you' to 'I am interested in forming a relationship with you'. If you approach your business, social and personal relationships with those thoughts in mind, you have a head start in displaying positive body language. Nonetheless, intrusive positive signals from you can be as bad as negative signals when there are no corresponding positive signals from the other person.

What is people's response to your body language?

The mirror effect which makes people simulate others' actions, intentions and emotions comes into play. When you display negative body language, your message to people is that you are not interested in creating a relationship based on the terms under consideration. In response, people may walk away from you, reject your proposal or reject your application in interviews. In short, they tend not to build a relationship with you. There is plenty at stake in the signals you display.

On the other hand, when they see positive body language, they are more likely to view you with openness and respond in the same vein. It all depends on the signals you display.

What then, are the signals through which we display our body language?

All of us display four signals to reflect our inner state of feeling. These signals are more likely to be in sync with our verbal communication when what we speak is true to our feelings or as in Rashmi's case, to be at variance with it. Her body language was completely at odds with her words.

Body language is one of the oldest forms of communication, and has evolved, growing increasingly complex as it comes to us from animals, birds and fish. To them, it's a matter of physical survival,

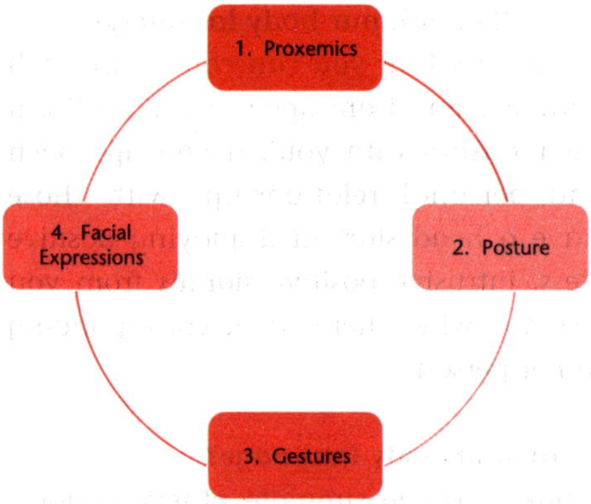

Signals of Body Language

to us it's a complex matter of survival in our social, business and personal spaces.

Adding to its depth and complexity is the fact that human body language is learned culturally and can carry different meanings among different regions, unlike animals which learn their behaviour by instinct and hence, display signals whose meanings generally remain the same.

As an element of first impressions, body language is one of the most difficult to control since it emerges directly from our emotions. It doesn't always say what you want it to say. It is a silent language through which you send and interpret the signals subconsciously. More likely than not, your body tells the truth even as your words speak different.

According to US Educational Psychologist, Albert Mehrabian who originally introduced a set of statistics behind verbal and non-verbal communication, the 7 per cent-38 per cent-55 per cent rule denotes our communication through words, tone and non-verbal behaviour through facial expressions respectively[1]. This is related to expressing feelings and attitudes. Many times, our action is not intended to communicate, yet it does, like yawning, showing possible disinterest.

Given its importance, it becomes important for you to understand the signals of body language and how they operate to create a negative or positive first impression.

1. PROXEMICS

Had the man facing Rashmi understood the science of proxemics, he would have known that he was standing within her personal space where she wasn't yet ready to accept him.

Proxemics is the study of distances from which people interact with one another. Introduced by anthropologist, Edward T Hall, it states that each of us lives within a bubble, sub-consciously desiring a certain amount of space around us. Maintain that distance and you leave a positive feeling. Move closer or farther and you may create a negative first impression.

While the intimate, personal, social and public spaces are clear enough, what is the proper distance for business space?

A good measure is the distance you require for a handshake, about 2 to 2.5 feet. That is a safe distance for business communication.

PROXEMICS — PERSONAL REACTION BUBBLES[2]

The distance within each type of space is shown below:

- Intimate distance for embracing, touching or whispering
  - Close phase — less than 6 inches (15 cm)
  - Far phase — 6 to 18 inches (15 to 46 cm)
- Personal distance for interactions among

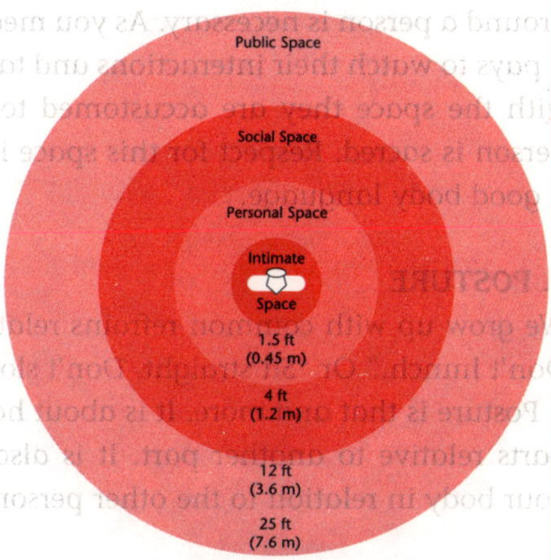

good friends or family members
  - Close phase — 1.5 to 2.5 feet (46 to 76 cm)
  - Far phase — 2.5 to 4 feet (76 to 120 cm)
- Social distance for interactions among acquaintances
  - Close phase — 4 to 7 feet (1.2 to 2.1 m)
  - Far phase — 7 to 12 feet (2.1 to 3.7 m)
- Public distance used for public speaking
  - Close phase — 12 to 25 feet (3.7 to 7.6 m)
  - Far phase — 25 feet (7.6 m) or more.

The actual distance maintained between two people is a cultural phenomenon. Cultures like those in the Middle-East require little space in comparison to Latin Americans, who in turn stand too close for the comfort of Europeans or North Americans.

In addition, individuals have personal preferences of the distance they would like to maintain with others. When this distance is breached, they may find it intrusive, even threatening. Hence, being aware of and respecting the requirements of space around a person is necessary. As you meet people of other cultures, it pays to watch their interactions and take their cue, leaving them with the space they are accustomed to. This bubble around the person is sacred. Respect for this space is the first pre-requisite for a good body language.

2. POSTURE

We grow up with common refrains related to posture, "Stand tall. Don't hunch." Or "Sit straight. Don't slouch."

Posture is that and more. It is about how you position your body parts relative to another part. It is also about how you position your body in relation to the other person.

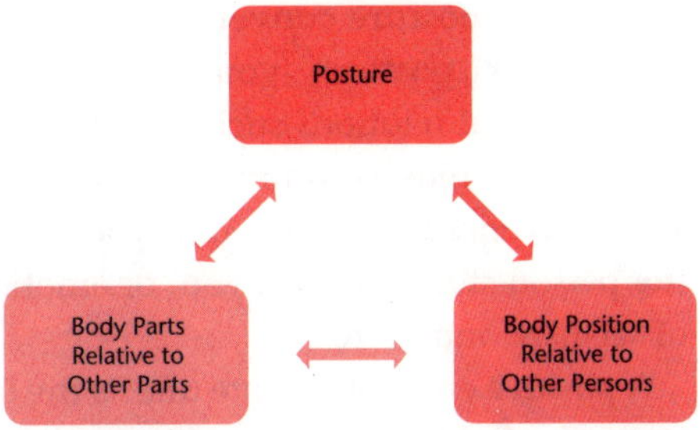

Rajat was making his presentation for the marketing campaign. While the others faced him, the head of finance was angled away, glancing intermittently at his laptop. Obviously, his attention was elsewhere. Although Rajat had in-principle approval from finance, the head could still come up with some stiff questions. Without the finance head understanding the objectives, the full preparation and expected results of the campaign, it would be a tough road ahead.

Rajat took note of this, pausing to gain the finance head's attention through the silence. He then asked him his opinion about a certain objective and its result. It required a pretty direct answer without ambiguity — a safe question in fact. Having caught his attention, Rajat proceeded with the presentation, maintaining eye contact with the finance head to retain his attention.

When listening to audience questions, particularly from the sales and product teams, Rajat found himself standing with his arms crossed and legs apart. It took a conscious effort to uncross his arms and take a more open stance. In doing so, he found that he was taking a less aggressive stance in responding to their questions. He also realized that since the campaign affected them, their concerns were genuine. What's more, the tougher the questions were now, the better the chances of plugging potential gaps in the campaign and the more successful the end result.

Facing the person frontally is like leaving the door to your house wide open, a welcome gesture. Crossing your legs, hands or ankles is assumed to indicate a locked door, that you have closed yourself to the person in front.

What does posture convey?

With your posture, you convey messages regarding your interpersonal relations such as, whether you like the other person or not. You may communicate personality traits like confidence, submissiveness, openness and your social standing in relation to the person standing with you, or emotions like fear, tension, sense of security and more[3].

A positive emotional state affects the body posture with a positive state of mind leading to positive postures. When you see a person with an erect bearing, you can easily see the sense of confidence in him. When he stands with an open stance, with the trunk exposed and facing you with a smile, it is a reflection of attention, warmth and welcome. Positive postures are fluid, powerful and restful without being overbearing. They attract people into your personal spaces.

On the other hand, a negative state of mind displays negative postures. Collapsed, drooped or hunched positions may depict dejection, disappointment or submission. When you turn slightly away from the person, you may indicate shyness or boredom. Hunching over and keeping arms and legs crossed may indicate hostility, unfriendliness and anxiety. Negative postures are characterized by short, stiff, erratic, fairly uncontrolled movements, indicating anxiety or being ill at ease. When others mirror this posture, it reinforces your own negative posture further and stimulates a vicious negative cycle.

Posture must be viewed in combination with other signals of body language since it could very well be just a matter of your health and physique rather than an indication of your inner state.

3. GESTURES

Hand gestures are linked to better speaking ability. According to a study at the University of Chicago, we think in two forms simultaneously when we speak. Speech and gesture go together[4].

From emphatic to descriptive, we have a range of gestures to add to our verbal messages. Through gestures, we show our displeasure, our enthusiasm and how strongly we feel, making the words come alive. Even if your heart is bursting with excitement, if you have a stiff, verbal form of communication with little body language or gestures to accompany it, your audience is at risk of thinking you are not interested in the subject.

Although you can learn the art of gestures to lend strength to your speech, evolving your own natural style is as important. But the gesture should not be allowed to distract the audience from your face. It breaks their eye contact. If you have just learned a gesture, it's best to work with it till it becomes natural, if not, there's the chance of it happening at the wrong time and hence becoming incongruent.

Before you build your repertoire of gestures, you need to know the answer to the question, are gestures universal?
Cultures vary widely in how they display and interpret gestures. The V for Victory indicated by raised index and middle fingers accepted in North America and many other cultures is considered rude in Italy when the back of the hand is shown. Thumbs up may mean a job well done in Western culture, but is an insult in the Middle-East, Latin America, Greece, Russia and West Africa. Middle-Eastern cultures also tend to be more expressive while Norwegians aren't known for vigorous gestures[5]. It pays to watch your hand gestures when in company of people from other cultures.

4. FACIAL EXPRESSIONS

It was Charles Darwin, Father of the Theory of Evolution, who discovered non-verbal communication clues[6] after he found interest in the similarities between humans and animals in expressing emotions through facial expressions.

Facial expressions that depict the seven universally recognized emotions are related to fear, anger, surprise, contempt, disgust, happiness and sadness. You portray many more expressions, ranging from concentration, confusion, desire to frustration, love and more.

Also present are micro expressions brought to the forefront by Paul Ekman. Those tiny expressions that flit across your face, seemingly too quick for people to register, but they leave their mark on the person in front.

Remain conscious of the way you feel and where you look. Your eyes and mouth are the most important features expressing your intent. A twisted smile indicates your mixed feelings or even sarcasm. Forced laughter indicates your nervousness and cooperation. A smile that never reaches your eyes is a dead giveaway that it isn't genuine.

The rule of thumb is to offer an open smile. When you find yourself slipping into negative facial expressions, watch your inner feelings and control the expression from there.

What do we communicate through our eye movement?

Eyes are the window to your soul. The performance of a great actor lies in his eyes. From looking directly into the eyes of the interviewer to gazing directly into your partner's eyes, eyes are an important factor in conveying the message.

You look away when you are disinterested. You do not meet the person's eyes when you lie or disagree with them. You might lower your eyes to show submissiveness or it indicates shyness. Or you may roll your eyes to show that the idea is incredulous. When you widen your eyes, if it isn't shock, you express interest. By blinking frequently, you show either excitement or that you are under pressure.

Knowing the signals of body language is fine, but how do I influence my body language? Without that, I have no control over first impressions.

Control over body language is more than skin deep. Since it is a reflection of your emotions, control depends on your emotional quotient, introduced by Dr Daniel Goleman. While looking within yourself is one side of the coin, the other side is to be able to relate to the person in front in order to school your emotions. As Dr Goleman advises, schooling your emotions[7] is a matter of learning the following:

- **Emotional Self-awareness:** Recognize your emotions and understand their causes. Recognize the difference between feelings and actions. You do not have to act on your negative feelings.
- **Managing Emotions:** Build tolerance to negative emotions like frustration and anger and the resultant actions like verbal put-downs and fights. This helps you ultimately in managing your emotions in a healthy way, building positive feels about yourself and lowering stress and anxiety.
- **Harnessing Emotions Productively:** Remain responsible. Carry self-control. Be less impulsive and focus on the task at hand.

The above three tasks are related to managing your emotions by managing yourself. The two tasks below are about relating to the person in front.

- **Empathy — Reading Emotions:** Take the other person's perspective. Build higher levels of empathy and sensitivity. Listen well to others.
- **Handling Relationships:** Analyze and understand relationships. Resolve conflicts and problems in relationships while remaining cooperative and helpful to others. Be considerate while remaining effective in your communication.

Going back to the example in the section on postures in which Rajat presented the marketing campaign, he had taken these two necessary steps to control his body language. He immediately corrected his negative, defensive stance. At the same time, he looked at it from the point of view of the team members and their genuine concerns. He saw the value of listening to their concerns with openness which itself became a positive reinforcement and his body language turned more positive and natural than if he had simply willed it to be so without putting himself in the others' shoes.

Question arises, if you intentionally correct your posture although it is at conflict with how you feel, does it work?

Dr Li Huang and Dr Adam Galinsky at North Western University, Illinois, in a study comparing the effects of posture on self-esteem, found a higher correlation between the two than between position of power and self-esteem. People who were told they had become managers, indicating an elevation to a position of power, scored lower in self-esteem than those who sat in expansive postures with legs spread wide and arms reaching outward[8]. In this case, the positive posture enhanced their self-esteem.

Straightening your body posture and opening up to the person in front not only conveys a positive message, it also has a positive impact on your mental state. As far as body language is concerned, although the signals take place unconsciously, being aware of the signal can help you control it to your advantage. This in turn affects your mental state positively, giving positive reinforcement.

Training yourself to greet openly and offering a firm handshake are individual elements and nothing about your personality can be sliced and looked at separately. The first impressions that the stranger is forming is a complex mix of elements. Make sure that in addition to correcting the signal, you correct your emotion too and remain empathetic to the person. This automatically corrects the other signals which you may not be aware of at that moment.

If not, they will remain in conflict, bringing your tower of impressions crashing down.

Etiquette

Read the word 'Etiquette' and the thought that springs to mind is of dining etiquette with its array of spoons, forks, knives and the like. But etiquette has a far wider meaning and carries far deeper consequences.

What is etiquette?

Etiquette is a code of behaviour that meets social norms. Sometimes, it seems so inflexible that we wonder why we need etiquette in the first place. But, etiquette is the code that makes life in society comfortable.

At the simplest level, it is nothing more than good manners. It helps us respect others' feelings, time, effort and personal need. It also tells us what to expect from others. If we had to constantly guess what the other person would do or how they would respond to a situation, our minds would be too preoccupied and the levels of stress will rise.

The basic and most important message you convey is 'I respect you'. But, when the interviewer is kept waiting a good ten minutes before you arrive, you are telling them, 'I do not respect you, the job or the company'. At the second level, you convey messages relevant to the occasion. By arriving on time, you are saying, 'I am interested in this job or this company' or 'This job and this company are priority to me'.

If it is a gift you send a thank you note for, you are saying, 'I appreciate the effort you have put into sending me this gift'.

When you treat people with respect, they think well of themselves. When they do that, they are more disposed to feel good about you and form positive first impressions.

Some have a concern. 'There seems to be etiquette for each little thing in the world. How do I learn everything?'

If you follow the rule of respect to others, it automatically means that you put others ahead of yourself and that is the fundamental code of etiquette. Although there will always be smaller details about how to behave, this rule covers most things.

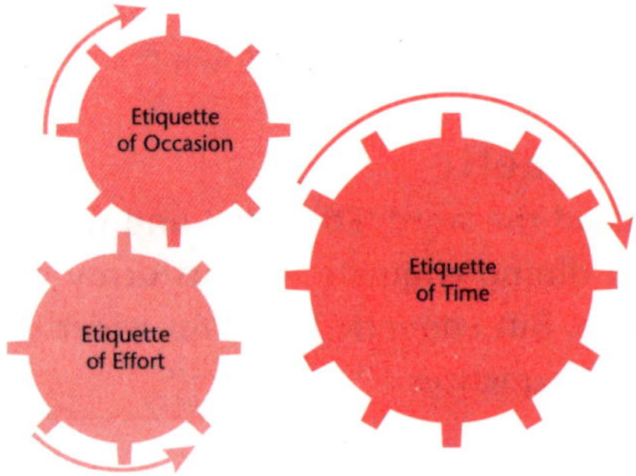

Parameters of Etiquette

For ease of understanding, we have grouped the codes of etiquette into three broad parameters based on what is expected of you.

Parameters of Etiquette

ETIQUETTE OF TIME

The etiquette of time is one of the most critical codes of etiquette. From arriving on time at office, conferences, meetings, parties to formal or informal visits, it is a measure of your respect for other's time.

Surekha, a mid-level finance executive has this to say, "Ours was a software firm which had begun operations in the USA. We had weekly calls with the US executives where we discussed issues. I was impressed with their sense of time.

Each Wednesday at 6.30pm Indian Standard Time (IST) when we had the call, they were on call a few minutes early. It's embarrassing to say that we would be there a few minutes after the scheduled time. It took me a few calls to discipline myself enough to dial in a few minutes early.

I was surprised when they later told me that they relied on me more than anyone else to get things done on time. I'm sure my presence on time helped."

When people extrapolate, they do so from the impressions they form of you. From watching Surekha be on time to extrapolating that she would make sure things were done on time was no surprise, and that is what happened.

ETIQUETTE OF EFFORT

From a simple thank you note, email or phone call, to offering something in return, these are an expression of your appreciation and gratitude for the thought and effort put in by others. It could be a gift, taking on your share of work when you are behind schedule or unwell, to giving you right-of-way on the road. Families, friends, acquaintances and business associates, each of them does a thing or two in your favour for which you need to follow through in thanking them.

"I hadn't really given much thought to what my mother-in-law thought of me, I mean, we had a fairly good relationship going, until she appreciated the trouble I had taken to make her sister's family's visit comfortable," says Namita.

"I would have thought it was part of the family duty, they were guests after all, but the fact that she recognized it made me realize that she hadn't taken me for granted. That helps in a relationship. Of course, we have our ups and downs, but now saying a 'thank you' comes more naturally to me when she takes care of my two-year-old.

I see many of my cousins take grand parents' help quite for granted, but I understand the fact that at her age, it is an effort for my mother-in-law. But, she does it with a smile and gives me my much needed break and I appreciate that."

ETIQUETTE OF OCCASION

This is the broadest parameter. The variety of occasions include business etiquette, social etiquette, family etiquette, dining etiquette, etiquette at marriages and while offering condolence at a death. It includes online etiquette, email etiquette, etiquette in visiting someone's home, public space etiquette that includes elevators, queues, road, and other public spaces, during travel and the many other situations we find ourselves in.

This is where one can get bogged down, but having respect for others helps you through most of these situations. For complicated rituals of etiquette in a new place or occasion, follow others' example or take the trouble to find the details, learn and act accordingly.

Sahil was a sociable person and often had socio-business gatherings many weekends at his home. Thanks to his wife's efforts, the gatherings were a success. Food was good and in plenty. The guests were made to feel comfortable.

Sahil on the other hand was quite blind to his guests. He would be the first to grab a drink or a plate of appetizers even before he offered it to the guests. In doing so, he revealed his true nature, self-centered to the point of being blind to others. It eventually showed up in a slowdown in his career. What was evident in his social life was extrapolated to his business life as well.

When it comes to our family, although we often tend to take family for granted, it pays to apply the same rules of respect, kindness and courtesy here too. The family is the most important part of our lives, and following these principles builds greater peace, support and relaxed feel at home.

What do you do when the other person breaks the code of etiquette to the point that it disturbs the audience or work at hand?

Business etiquette demands many things, giving your full attention to the speaker, being concise and polite, respecting the company culture, privacy, people and more.

Kanchan, a client-servicing executive, once found her audience engaging in a conversation while she made her presentation. "Rather than continue with my presentation, I stood silent, waiting for them to put an end to their conversation. It had its effect," she said.

If it is your seniors or colleagues breaching the standards of etiquette, there's a way of making things known. This applies to interviews too. When you take a firm stand without going overboard, you come across as polite yet firm, which is a positive characteristic to display.

In conclusion, even if you don't remember the details of etiquette, remember these three things — respect, kindness and courtesy. Make sure that your actions reflect this attitude. They put people at ease and help create positive first impressions and build future relationships.

REFERENCES

1 http://www.kaaj.com/psych/smorder.html

2 http://en.wikipedia.org/wiki/Proxemics

3 http://en.wikipedia.org/wiki/Posture_(psychology)

4 http://totalcommunicator.com/eyes_article.html

5 http://www.buzzle.com/articles/hand-gestures-and-their-meanings.html

6 http://www.netplaces.com/body-language/the-evolution-of-body-language/survival-of-the-fittest.htm

7 Emotional Intelligence - Why it can matter more than IQ, by Dr. Daniel Goleman

8 http://www.economist.com/node/17899714

SO FAR

- Body language is an expression of your emotions and personality traits.
- Positive messages you can convey through body language include 'I am open to you' or 'I am interested in forming a relationship with you'.
- The mirror effect aids people in responding to you based on your body language.
- Signals of body language include proxemics, posture, gestures and facial expressions.
- Proxemics is the distance from which you interact with people and includes intimate, personal, social, public spaces.
- Posture is your body position relative to other parts as well as your body position relative to other persons.
- Hand gestures must reflect your style without being distracting.
- Facial expressions depict your emotions. Watch your inner feelings and control the expression from there. Eye movement is an important component of facial expressions as eyes are the window to your soul.
- Emotional quotient determines how well you control your body language through emotional self-awareness, managing emotions, harnessing emotions productively, empathy and handling emotions positively.
- Positive posture enhances your self-esteem.
- Etiquette is about manners and is based on respect, kindness, courtesy.
- The message you convey with etiquette is 'I respect you'.
- Etiquette falls within three broad parameters — etiquette of time, effort and occasion.

Chapter 7

Vocal Communication – Engaging With Opening Conversations

The most important thing in communication is hearing what isn't said.

— Peter F Drucker

We had just begun with the session on vocal communication in our programme for image management and I asked the class a question, "What do you think is meant by the term vocal communication?"

"It is about what we say, isn't it?" said one.

"It is speaking with good diction."

"Knowing the right words."

"Being able to convey what you want to say the way you want others to hear it."

The last response got us close to what vocal communication is all about. And there we began.

"What many want to do," I said to the class, "when they want to perfect their vocal communication, is to know the right things to say. Understand that the purpose of vocal communication is to say things the way you want others to hear it. When you look at it this way, you will find that there is a lot more to it than just words."

This classroom discussion is representative of what many ask us, "Why do you call it vocal communication and not verbal communication?"

The answer lies in the message you convey when you speak. If all the messages you convey are based on just the words you speak, life would be robotic. Think of the last movie you watched. What if the actor said his dialogues in a monotone? How engaging would that be? How much involvement would you have with the character or the movie itself? This is true in real life too.

Just as the actor has a script that tells him the dialogue and the actor recites the dialogue in a manner unique to himself based on his perception of the role, so it is with you in real life roles. The only difference is that your script is original. Each time you speak out, even if it's just a "Hello," you have your own unique way of saying it.

At the same time, the actor is emoting through his body language — the proxemics, his posture, gestures, facial expressions and eye contact. Each of these signals combines to cause an effect on the audience.

With these efforts, the individual is conveying his message through two senses: the auditory — sense of hearing and the visual — sense of sight.

Verbal and Vocal Communication: Factors of Communication

Now, within these senses, three factors are involved in the delivery of your dialogue and how your audience perceives it:

1. Verbal Communication — What You Say
2. Vocal Communication — How You Say It
3. Visual Communication — What You Show

It is the combination of these factors, carrying verbal, vocal and visual signals, that conveys your message to your audience.

This is still a one-way street. The actor has no way of knowing the audience response to his dialogue. But, most real life situations involve face-to-face conversations where you can gauge the audience response and fine tune your message accordingly. The audience can range from one in the case of one-to-one conversations, to thousands in the case of public speaking. So the fourth factor is:

4. How Your Audience Responds

Being able to fine-tune your words, your intonation and your body language based on audience response helps you create positive first impressions.

We shall use the term vocal communication as the overall title when referring to how you communicate through speech since our focus will be on this element.

Factors of Vocal Communication

1. WHAT YOU SAY

The classroom may provide a good example of how boring things can get as the teacher simply talks and the student listens. It is in classes of those teachers who draw the students into the lesson through questions, stories, a bit of humour or some theatrics and practical involvement that students perk up, even the disinterested back benchers.

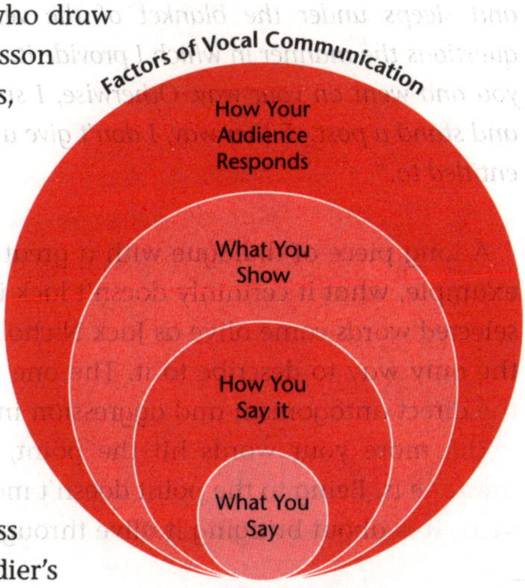

Take Jack Nicholson's dialogue towards the end of the movie *A Few Good Men* where he is on the witness stand for the trial of a soldier's death under his command. In the final court scene all he needed to say was, "Marine defense life is a tough life. If men are not treated with great toughness, they will not have the preparedness to defend the country." Straightforward words provide meaning, but they come nowhere close to touching the audience's heart.

What he actually said was, "… Son, we live in a world that has walls. And those walls have to be guarded by men with guns. Who's gonna do it? You? You, Lt. Weinberg? I have a greater responsibility than you can possibly fathom. You weep for Santiago and you curse the marines. You have that luxury. You have the luxury of not knowing what I know: That Santiago's death, while tragic, probably saved lives. And my existence, while grotesque and incomprehensible to you, saves lives.

You don't want the truth. Because deep down, in places you don't talk about at parties, you want me on that wall. You want me there. We use words like honor, code, loyalty...we use these words as the backbone to a life spent defending something. You use 'em as a punchline. I have neither the time nor the inclination to explain myself to a man who rises and sleeps under the blanket of the very freedom I provide, then questions the manner in which I provide it. I'd prefer you just said thank you and went on your way. Otherwise, I suggest you pick up a weapon and stand a post. Either way, I don't give a damn what you think you're entitled to."

A long piece of dialogue with a great bit of theatrics, but as an example, what it certainly doesn't lack is the punch. The carefully selected words come alive as Jack Nicholson spews them out, that's the only way to describe to it. The one thing we advise against is the direct antagonism and aggression in the dialogue.

The more your words hit the point, the more impactful your message is. Being to the point doesn't mean reciting a statement of facts. It is about bringing it alive through the words themselves.

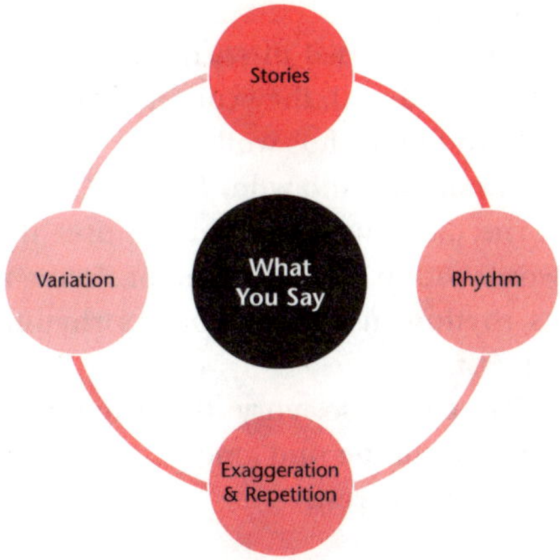

What would be your choice of words to bring your speech alive?
Stories, the natural rhythm of the languages you speak, exaggeration, repetition and variation are all effective methods to bring your words alive when you speak. Use them judiciously and you will build a great dialogue that keeps the audience involved. Words can thus be brought alive, performing the job of effective communication for you. They make sure that people remember what you said and form a positive impression of you.

Taking Nicholson's piece of dialogue, let's look at each in turn:

Stories

"Son, we live in a world that has walls. And those walls have to be guarded by men with guns." — With this, he creates a clear picture of walls and threats on the other side of the walls. A story is a picture you create in the person's mind. And a picture is worth a thousand words.

"..a man who rises and sleeps under the blanket of the very freedom I provide.." — A clear image emerges, of a person who is secure and at peace with the use of the word blanket *as a metaphor for* protection.

People find it difficult to retain lengthy arguments and facts. A simile or a metaphor can do as well as a story does. A single line is capable of evoking a clear image. So keep it simple.

Rhythm

The words used in each language have a rhythm of their own. When used well, they can make your speech captivating.

"..world that has walls.."

"...not knowing what I know.."

The dialogue in the movie uses this natural rhythm by using words with a similar sound or rhyme to them. Just as music varies its rhythm, use of language's rhythm helps you build audience interest.

You can also vary the rhythm with questions, alternating between shorter and longer sentences and effective pauses to retain audience interest.

Exaggeration, Repetition and Variation

Effective speakers often choose words that exaggerate what they aim to say. They use repetition while varying the words to convey the same message with emphasis.

"..Who's gonna do it? You? You, Lt. Weinberg?.."

There's an element of exaggeration in his accusation as well as repetition in the way the questions are asked. He is not looking for an answer, but this is effective in retaining interest. At the same time, the questions come as a variation in the middle of statements, changing the rhythm of the dialogue.

How is this helpful during first impressions? you might ask.
Just as the first paragraph is the critical component in writing, so it is with your speech. It is where you begin. And then where you carry on from there.

Think of the situation where you have introduced yourself to a group at the dinner party. Your opening conversation is like the label on the package. Visualize row upon row of bright packages in eye-catching colours on the supermarket shelves. Right in the middle of this stands a single dull, grey package. What is more likely to happen is that the customer will not notice it, or if she does, it would be just a passing glance.

Each of these factors — stories, rhythm, exaggeration, repetition, variation help you make strong opening conversations. They are also a strong component of regular conversations and presentations.

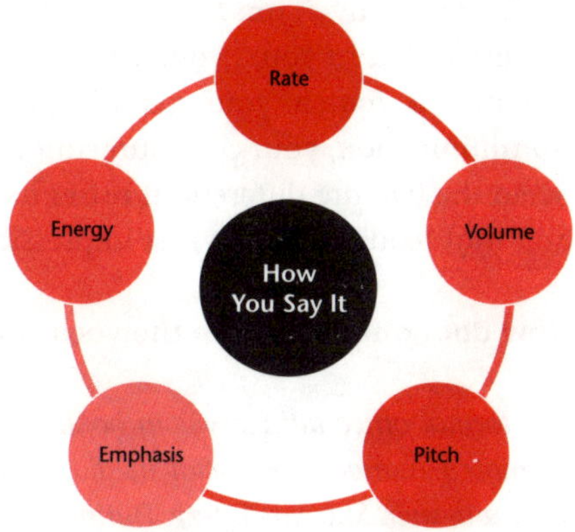

2. HOW YOU SAY IT

Each of you is unique in how you speak. That is the reason why, even if the words are garbled, you can make out the person at the end of the phone, if they are familiar to you. It is your rate, that is, the speed at which you speak, your volume, pitch, emphasis and your energy that makes the difference.

To give compelling speeches, effective speakers are known to modulate their voices, speed up their rate of speech or slow down, raise the volume or lower it and change the pitch according to the content.

Then there is the matter of the energy with which you speak. People tend to gather around those who are expressive and exude energy. However verbose, if the content is accompanied by a tired tone, this vocal cue conveys the real meaning to the listener.

The words you speak might be innocuous, but vocal factors give your speech different meanings. The result can be an exclamation, a question or a statement of acknowledgement, sarcasm, humour, anger, happiness, or a host of other meanings, attitudes and emotions.

When you say "I am happy" or "I am interested in this job" or "I am interested in you," your vocal tone conveys your true feelings. When you match your verbal communication with the vocal communication, your communication becomes more effective. But, when the two are different, it raises a conflict in the listener's mind and that leads to a poor first impression.

How does one modulate the vocal factors?

The formal office dinner was in honor of the visiting CEO. As the newly promoted manager of social media, it was Kanika's first invitation to such a dinner. She was jittery. During a conversation, the CEO asked her what she thought of the competitor's social media campaign in response to the recent product recalls they had to make.

Kanika found herself panicking. She began speaking at a speed that even her colleagues would find it difficult to follow. The CEO was a foreign national and in all her calls to the US team, she knew enough to slow down to make up not just for the lack of visual element, but also for the difference in diction.

She took a deep breath and continued more slowly. "It is a black mark, but they handled it right," she said. "They did the right things." Then she started ticking off the points on her fingers that held the wine glass. "One, they were on the social media within a half-hour of the breaking news, stating that they were looking into the matter. Two, they did get back with a response, a solution this time within an hour. Three, a 24-hour, two-person team, responding to public questions. Did they stop at that? No, their PR machinery was up and running, talking to print and online media. Did they leave the bloggers out? Or leave them for the last? Not at all. A parallel team was writing to bloggers and giving them the story first hand, sometimes, responding to posts that were coming up already."

The CEO nodded, talking more about their own company's social media strategy. It was a lengthy conversation for a dinner party.

What did Kanika do right?

- For all her panic, she observed her audience — the CEO.
- She immediately slowed down her rate of speech. Her volume, never very high, was soft in any case.
- She used a question-answer format to vary her pitch.
- She numbered the points of her speech. In addition to showing her clarity of thought and experience, it also gave her the time to insert pauses into what she said.
- She placed emphasis at the right intervals.

From starting conversations, to presentations, to public speaking on stage, each of these vocal factors brings your speech to life. Absence of these factors can cause your speech to become robotic while excessive use can make you sound like you are in a stage drama. For most of us, our vocal style in our business, social, private and public lives rests somewhere in the middle.

How do the rate, volume and pitch vary on different occasions?

In our business lives, our voice does not range across a wide band of rate, volume and pitch. Yet, good speakers use these factors of vocal communication to convey passion and energy, keeping the audience involved.

Take for example the speeches of famous people, like that of Steve Jobs at the Stanford University. You would find that they use the factors of vocal communication, that is, the rate, volume, pitch with the right emphasis at key points to retain audience interest. When it comes to speeches at product launches and sales meets, you would find that there is plenty of energy in addition to these factors to heighten the excitement and quicken the pace of the launch or increase the sales effort.

In our social lives, although there is a difference between the formal and highly casual events, these lives in general are witness to higher variation in voice than in our business lives. Given the fact that we tend to be free with ourselves in our personal lives, the variation in voice is the highest here among these three lives. But, here too the variation is subject to the occasion.

No two lives are the same for different people. So the effect varies. But from what we have seen, as you move from business to social to personal lives, the variation in voice is higher. With public speaking on the other hand, whether it is presentations or speeches to an audience of a few or numbering in the thousands, the variation in voice is higher. How you vary each factor and leverage them depends on your audience too.

3. WHAT YOU SHOW

We have explained in Chapter — 6, Body Language & Etiquette — Managing How Your Body Talks, that body language emerges from your inner feelings and can often be at variance with what you say. This is particularly true when your words mask your attitude and feelings, which is why lie detectors came into being in the first place.

Often you would find a guest appreciating your effort in hosting the party, saying, "The arrangements were perfect. It was a great occasion," but you are still left with the feeling that they didn't mean what they said. The tone could be flat, revealing a lack of feeling behind the words. It sounds like she was merely being polite.

Others have an exaggerated way of thanking you. This too need not be taken as the real intent. They may have schooled their tone for such an exaggeration, because etiquette demands it. That's when you watch the body language.

Your body can be a dead giveaway when you speak in conflict with your attitude and feelings. People in your business, social or personal lives are watching you at the same time that they are listening to you. Make sure you are in control of your emotions and your attitudes. This is how you make sure that the visual cues match the verbal and vocal cues, creating a positive first impression.

4. HOW YOUR AUDIENCE RESPONDS

A critical element in verbal and vocal communication is the opening conversation. Finding common interests to create a bond with a stranger will make it easier for the stranger to continue the conversation with you. Shared interests are a mutually binding phenomenon.

Going further, what you say has a lot to do with who the audience is. Knowing the people you are about to face is the first step to speaking to the audience. This helps you in selecting the right topics, words and tone.

Ashit, a software programmer, worked on the Facebook app for the space games his company had introduced recently. Within a group of programmers at a conference, his speech discussed at length the rackspace they required for development and testing, the programme they used and, the benefits of HTML 5 vs Native Apps when it came to mobile apps and so on.

At a social gathering however, when someone asked him what he did at work, he said, "My company creates Facebook apps. We've just done that hot app for space games." The conversation picked up from there. Completely non-technical, it was about the game itself rather than what went behind it.

From the choice of topic to choice of words, the kind of stories you tell, what you emphasize, your rate, volume and pitch, each of these elements depends on who your audience is. Just as Kanika had slowed the speed of her speech, or as Ashit had changed the topic of conversation, knowing your audience beforehand prepares you for what they expect and what they are comfortable with.

A few vocal sounds are learned, others are instinctive, as researchers found in a study of the sounds made by deaf people. Sounds like relief and amusement were easily recognized by hearing individuals. This is instinctive learning since deaf people could not have learned from any one. Other vocal sounds like triumph, could be cultural[1] — the sounds expressed by the deaf people for triumph were not decipherable to the hearing individuals. This led researchers to conclude that the sounds that are not learned by instinct, differ across cultures.

Some cultures are used to well-modulated speech patterns. Others have a louder volume and greater variation in pitch. If you don't know the details prior to the meeting or party, watch and learn. Your audience gives plenty of cues as to what is comfortable and what is not. Let's suppose you are not sure if your volume is too high for the party, watch the audience for their reaction. From lowering their voice, to leaning away from you, to excusing themselves from the group, they give you plenty of cues. Watch them and you can make the change in time.

So be aware of your audience, observe them and fine tune your verbal, vocal and visual signals to create positive first impressions.

REFERENCE

1 http://www.scientificamerican.com/podcast/episode.cfm?id=some-nonverbal-vocal-communication-10-11-17

SO FAR

- Communication is more than just words. It involves four factors, involving verbal, vocal and visual cues:
    - What you say — Choose your words carefully incorporating stories, the natural rhythm of the language, exaggeration, repetition and variation to convey the right meaning with impact.
    - How you say — Your rate, volume, pitch, emphasis and energy convey a subtle, yet strong message.
    - What you show — Your body language reveals your emotions. Be careful when your body language is at variance with what you say.
    - How your audience responds — Be aware of how your audience responds. It helps you make changes to your vocal communication.
- Find common interests for successful opening conversations.

Chapter 8

Who Am I?

If you continue to do what you have always done, you will continue to get what you have always gotten.

— Old Chinese Saying

Kaahini wanted to learn how she could create positive first impressions. "You don't know what it is like to be at the negative end of things," she moaned. "Always."

We asked her to elaborate.

"I never get selected at the first few interviews. If there are two people applying for the job, you can be sure I am the one who won't make it. Out of a dozen interviews I attend, there is one middling one that I finally get. And that happens after sacrificing a hike that I should be getting or I would be given work a level below what I am looking for."

Was it just a matter of how Kaahini projected herself? Was it that she lacked the confidence? Or was it her performance?

Words continued to tumble out of her without any prompting. "When I go to parties, you can guess where I stand. I am the plant in the corner, watching the world go by."

Why do people with so much potential, struggle to realize that potential? Like Kaahini, many feel that the world doesn't do them

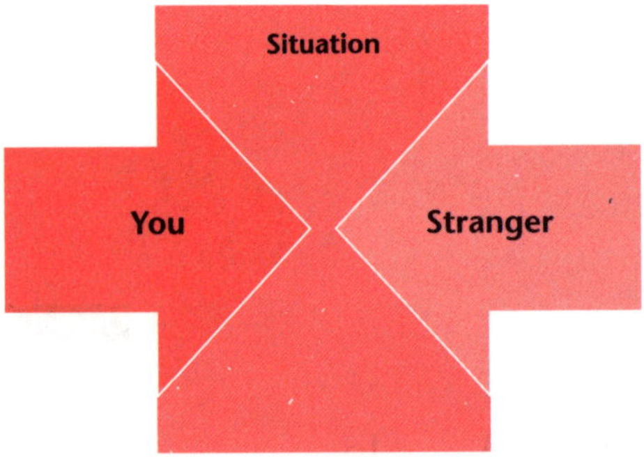

justice. They feel the world does not understand them nor see their potential.

But, truth is, the first impressions you create and your relationship with the world depends on two factors — you and the stranger. Forming the backdrop is the situation, which influences the behaviour of these two factors. The first impression formed and the potential relationship that can be built eventually is weak or strong, depending on how you and the stranger respond to each other in a given situation. Further, it is in your hands to ensure that the first impression created in the stranger's mind is positive.

While it looks like a straightforward interaction, it is anything but that.

Let us consider you, for instance. Innumerable permutations and combinations of possibilities exist based on your attitudes, perceptions and the personality that you display to different people under different situations. Similarly, the stranger brings in many factors like background, knowledge, experience and preferences.

The mirror effect which we had discussed in Chapter — 6, Body Language & Etiquette — Managing How Your Body Talks, comes into play too, making the stranger reflect and respond to the image you project. When you remain aware of this effect, you realize that you are the driver of the situation, giving you greater control over the first impressions you create.

Since change always begins with the self, in this chapter, we go into detail about you and how you can create positive first impressions by knowing yourself, taking feedback and projecting yourself harmoniously.

As Larry Bossidy and Ram Charan, the famed authors of Confronting Reality: Doing What Matters to Get Things Right say, "Self-awareness gives you the capacity to learn from your mistakes as well as your successes. It enables you to keep growing[1]."

That brings us to the question, "Who are You?" When we pose this question, our students struggle to answer. The question is not as direct as it seems. Most answer it with just their name and career.

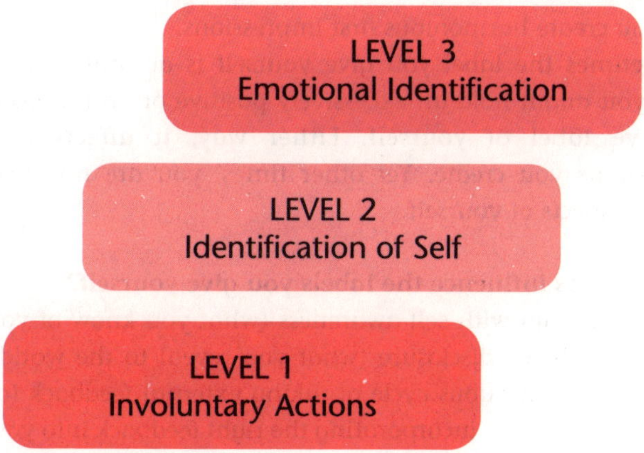

Levels of Identification

At the survival level are the acts our body performs without our conscious thought — breathing, heartbeat, digestion and so on — the involuntary actions.

At level 2 is the conscious identification of oneself. This is where we answer the "Who are You" question with our names and titles, "My name is Rita," "I am a customer service manager," the information we give to strangers.

At level 3 is the concept of emotional identification. Here, we identify our feelings and our personality. We may label ourselves with our traits, for example, "I am an extrovert," "I am shy," "I fear social situations." But, more often, these labels are evident from what we say: our stories, conversations, and responses that are disclosed through the elements of first impressions, clothing, grooming, body language, including etiquette and vocal communication. With each of these elements, we reveal ourselves and our feelings to the world in ways that sometimes we are blind to.

This is the level that can tell you what you need to know about yourself and how you project yourself. Knowing the labels you give yourself and making a conscious effort to project the right ones is how you create harmonious first impressions.

Sometimes the label you give yourself is accurate. But, other times you might hold an excessively positive or an unreasonably negative label of yourself. Either way, it affects the first impressions you create. Yet other times, you are not aware of certain aspects of yourself.

What factors influence the labels you give yourself?

The labels begin with self-awareness (what you know of yourself) and end with self-disclosure (what you reveal to the world). The process is a continuous cycle of taking external feedback (of how people see you) and incorporating the right feedback into your self-awareness and self-disclosure.

The way you handle this entire process is determined by your self-esteem and self-mastery. These factors strongly influence whether you give yourself a positive or a negative label. These 5 factors make up The Cycle of Image Projection.

The Cycle of Image Projection

What you build with self-esteem is respect for yourself and the confidence to help you navigate your business, social and personal lives with ease. But self-esteem without self-mastery is inadequate and can easily lead to arrogance and pride that, in turn, lead to negative first impressions.

Self-mastery is the result of your emotional quotient which we described in Chapter—7 on Body Language, Including Etiquette: Managing How Your Body Talks. It helps you learn emotional self-awareness, manage your emotions and harness your emotions productively. At the same time, it helps you build empathy, read people's emotions accurately and handle relationships well. All these are critical components that build upon your intellectual and work skills and bring out your full potential.

Self-mastery is also the underlying component that helps you take feedback effectively. It determines how self-aware you are, what your self-esteem is and what you disclose to the world. It gives you control over yourself, makes you empathetic, helps you overcome frustrations and be ready to work with others. Because of its influence over all the other factors, it is the critical factor that helps in creating positive and strong first and lasting impressions.

In this chapter, we shall deal with feedback only to the extent that it influences the internal factors. We shall elaborate it in the next chapter when we discuss how the world sees you and why it sees you the way it does.

The question that arises related to self-awareness is, how do I know who I am? How do I know if my labels are correct?

Each of us has a sense of who we are, our self-awareness. But it is nowhere near the complete reality. There are parts of us that are known to others but not to us and other parts that remain unknown to both. At the same time, we try to keep some parts hidden from others. When we group them, they fall into 3 categories:

1. Who you are — Which you know
2. Who you are — Which you don't know
3. Who you could be

When you recognize these aspects, you strengthen your ability to project the image that creates strong and positive first impressions.

1. WHO YOU ARE — WHICH YOU KNOW

Of all the inner aspects that make up who we are, we know some while we remain blind to other aspects. Among the ones that we know of ourselves, there are the positive as well as the negative aspects.

Often during our training and consulting, we see people assume the mistaken belief that how they see themselves is how the world sees them. Unfortunately, that's not true. We've also seen them live under the hope that the world cannot see their negative side.

If you live under these beliefs, you are leaving things to chance. The world sees what is on display. Unless you make a conscious effort to exhibit your positives and limit your negatives, you are allowing the world to see random aspects of yourself. So, people are likely to remain blind to some of your most important positive aspects while they might be witness to the negative aspects. It is for you to consciously project the positives that you know about yourself so that the world judges you in the best light.

How does what you project to the world help in first impressions?

Positive disclosures are traits which people can relate to. The larger the number of positive disclosures, the more receptive people are to you. The world can relate better to you as it gets to know more of these aspects. This is the area where positive first impressions are formed and communication is clear with the audience dealing with you.

The right way to form positive first impressions is to expand the positive aspects that the world can see. You make the conscious effort to project what you want to reveal to make the right first impressions.

How do you expand the positives that the world can see?

The answer lies in showing the positives selectively or minimizing the negatives on display. Take a deep look at the positive aspects that you know of yourself. Some of these remain hidden from the stranger's view for lack of attention to the four elements. Understand the stranger and their expectations based on the occasion. Make the conscious effort to meet their expectations through the four elements. Also, check your state of mind. Make sure that a negative event during the day has not affected your mood and thereby the image you project of yourself.

At the same time, look at the aspects of yourself that you hide deep within yourself, trying not to show them to the world. There is little self-disclosure with items that you are uncomfortable with. So the question arises, why do you try to keep them hidden? There are three reasons to it, each requiring a different solution to expand the area the world can see.

- **Holding back Emotional Identification Information:** Typically, with a stranger, you reveal very little of yourself, as opposed to someone who's known you for years and is close to you, where there is a lot more self-disclosure. In forming positive first impressions, the time to disclose is now. While you are revealing just the level 2 information related to identification of the self, people are already forming first impressions based on non-verbal cues related to level 3 emotional identification information. These are cues that you tend to reveal even without your knowledge. Expanding the area that the world can see involves bringing these unconscious cues into the conscious area to help you project the image that is true to you.

- **Hiding Negative Emotions:** More importantly, vulnerability to negative emotions like fear, shame, anger, jealousy and a concern over how people would judge you if they knew the real you, makes you hide these aspects. On the other hand, you tend to disclose positive emotions easily. When you are happy for a person, you are ready to reveal your happiness. When you are confident about the success of a project or simply about yourself, you are happy to talk about it. More often than not, it is present in the ease with which you carry yourself. It is the negative aspects that you begin to hide. When you fear failure in the project or worse still, if you consider yourself a failure, it is more likely that you will hide it. You are also likely to keep your negative reaction to a person's behaviour under wraps than tell them about it, particularly when the stakes are high, like a friendship, a job interview, a promotion, or a family relationship.
- **Hiding Unrelated Tribes:** Each of us belongs to many tribes or groups. People relate best to those who belong to their tribes. When you disclose information about a tribe that you share with the stranger, you create a positive first impression because now, the stranger can relate to you. On the other hand, when you disclose the fact that you belong to an unrelated tribe, the stranger is likely to form a negative or weak first impression at best. Either they view this unrelated tribe negatively, or it is not the tribe that they want you to belong to. The result is that they cannot build a relationship with you.

What can we do about negative emotions and unrelated tribes?
The truth about hiding an aspect of self is that sooner or later it shows up in the innumerable visual and verbal cues that you tend to reveal without realizing. This happens particularly through your

body language and vocal communication. So the answer to the question is not to hide negative emotions, but to work towards minimizing them.

When it comes to negative emotions like fear, shame, anger and so on, you need to work on them. There is no easy path. Take a deep look at negative thoughts and feelings. Which of these are you keeping under wraps? Do you think you are ugly? Not pretty enough? Not smart enough? Not in control? Afraid of failure? Are you envious of a colleague? Do you worry that you will not be able to complete the task? Each of these feelings and emotions that you try to hide do not remain hidden. They become visible through your clothing, grooming, body language and vocal communication. Hence, you need to work through these feelings by enhancing your self-mastery. The resultant control over your feelings and emotions will help you minimize negative emotions from being projected inadvertently.

Other times, you may carry negative feelings towards a person. Are you upset at a colleague who never delivers? Do you get furious with the one-sided arguments of a friend? If these are recurring aspects, disclosing them in as neutral a way as possible helps you resolve them at the root rather than struggle unsuccessfully to hide them.

When we belong to unrelated tribes, the solution lies not in hiding them, but in focusing on highlighting the tribes you share with the stranger. Focus on the unrelated tribes in such cases is automatically minimized. But, remember, the idea is to let the stranger see more of the positive you by minimizing what you withhold from them.

What can possibly happen when you hide information about yourself?

When you consciously hide information like a negative trait rather than correct the trait itself, people often sense that information is being withheld. Your body language and vocal communication may inadvertently reveal what you have been trying to hide. In such cases, the result is a negative first impression which leads to an unsatisfactory relationship, if there is one at all. Hence it is necessary to correct the trait where necessary and possible.

Sometimes, you may carry high self-esteem and when not coupled with self-mastery, it could result in a disclosure of arrogance and a superiority complex. You might think you have hidden it well, but it reveals itself in superciliousness, loudness or unwarranted aggression. Potential work, social and family relationships suffer. If they are formed out of compulsion, the relationship will remain stunted and may eventually break.

Anuj had plenty of things that he knew he could not reveal. One stands out for its harsh repercussions.

Coming as he did from a company where aggression and table thumping was the norm to get across one's point, he knew it did not fit into the culture at the company he was interviewing with. Trouble was, he had become part of the culture of his current company and in heated discussions got quite aggressive.

Anuj knew this and took care to keep it hidden at the interview. Although all went well at the interview, three months into the new job, at one of the product meetings during a discussion about upcoming product features, Anuj's voice rose until it drowned all the other voices and it was a full two minutes before he realized it and stopped abruptly. It was as if he was speaking to make his voice heard above a loud noise, suddenly the noise stops and he continued as loud as if he was on stage.

If that was all that he did, things might have continued to work well. But he made a couple of personal attacks at the product team and that cost him his job. At his new company, things were conducted with more decorum and personal attacks of any kind were severely frowned upon. He got his termination letter within two days.

When certain key aspects remain hidden because you are unaware of your strengths or are reluctant to make a conscious effort to disclose these aspects, you stand to lose since it prevents people from forming positive first impressions. If you do not disclose critical aspects of yourself, for example, your straightforwardness, your eagerness and your diligence, people do not have all the right information to judge you by.

Let's go back to Kaahini's example. Kaahini was a wallflower during social occasions, because she was an introvert who took very long to open up to people. During social occasions, this ended up with her listening rather than contributing to the conversation. Even when the other person talked about things that she could relate to, she would not volunteer information about herself and conversation stagnated.

Conversations are a two-way street. One speaks, the other responds, and hence the conversation goes back and forth. If one person fails to respond, the conversation peters out.

With very little self-disclosure from Kaahini, people were reluctant to extend themselves and they moved on.

Something similar happened in her interviews. Kaahini never liked getting into arguments or having to defend herself. So, she preferred talking about her projects, the factual detail, and would not willingly elaborate her opinions and judgments which were a necessary part of the evaluation for the position of a manager. This revealed her in a poor light, leading to rejection. Eventually, the jobs she did get put her back at her original operational level work.

When you don't make a conscious effort at self-disclosure, you are leaving your image to chance. Make the choice. For some, like Kaahini, it is largely a matter of making a conscious effort to disclose their strengths. For others, the choice involves hard work internally to minimize the negative traits, as in Anuj's case.

2. WHO YOU ARE — WHICH YOU DON'T KNOW

Psychology is in many ways, the blind side of ourselves. We don't know much of what goes on in our mind.

Here we discuss those aspects that are unknown to you, but known to others. As discussed in the earlier chapters, these aspects are constantly being revealed to the world through the elements of clothing, grooming, body language or vocal cues while you remain unaware of it.

Who you are is constantly being projected. And it is through these four elements that it happens.

Why is your blind side important?

Many positive first impressions fail here. You believe that you are projecting the image of a competent, empathetic, open and confident professional. But, the stranger, who could be an interviewer, acquaintance or future family member, sees something else entirely. They may be forming the first impression of you as an indecisive, unsure, withdrawn individual or one who is difficult to please.

People with large blind sides to themselves are unaware of how people perceive them. They are either unable to read the feedback that comes their way or are unable to process the feedback and learn from it.

Vineet was a senior manager in the marketing department and was in charge of organizing events. He was always on the move, making sure that things went on smoothly. In meetings and long discussions, he had the habit of tapping his feet constantly. People often formed the impression that he was impatient or bored through this body language.

Secondly, Vineet was meticulous about planning and organizing the events. But when it came to his clothing, he wasn't as careful. His suits were well-tailored, but his tie was always slightly askew and his socks would sag. This spoiled an otherwise neat appearance. On first sight,

Vineet gave the impression of a person who didn't care much about what others thought of him. It also projected an image of someone who is careful about the big things, but paid little attention to the details.

Seeking feedback from others is how you resolve your blind side, according to the Johari Window introduced by Joseph Luft and Harry Ingham[2]. It gives you greater understanding of yourself. It also resolves the gap between what they see vs what you think they see. This in turn helps you not just in forming positive first impressions, but also, in improving existing relationships.

It isn't always your weaknesses that you are blind to. At times, people see your strengths more clearly than you do. This happens when you don't know that they exist or refuse to see your strengths for fear of failure in taking a new path. Here too, seeking other's feedback helps you become more self-aware. What is really important is that it has the capacity to raise your self-esteem, an important factor in creating powerful positive first impressions.

Anita's uncle once told her, "You are like the Lord Hanuman. You don't know your own strength." They were discussing Anita's potential as a singer.

Anita was on the point of giving up singing as a career in the interest of having a more stable career for herself. She was about to turn to becoming yet another engineer in the family and "sing on the side", *as they put it.*

None in her family had anything to do with music. All engineers and doctors, they looked askance at her desire to make singing her career. She was a good singer who put her heart into the music and worked long hours with dedication. She had the potential to become a great singer. What she needed was the belief in herself.

We often carry self-defeating thoughts like "I am ugly," "I am not good enough," "I am not smart," or as in the case of Anita, "What if I fail?"

You look at the world and hear what you believe the world is telling you. But, that negative thought may not be what the world is thinking at all.

When you think, "I am ugly," the world in all probability hasn't noticed a thing. On the contrary, the world may think you have grace and poise.

When you think you aren't good enough, your boss may trust you to see the project to completion.

When you think you aren't smart, your peers may be waiting for your advice.

So, don't assume you know the world's view. Be open to feedback.

Mallika was shy and apprehensive about social gatherings where she didn't know many people. She felt her dress was never right, that she was not good looking, that she was too heavy. She felt that as a baker who operated from home, she could not make smart conversation.

She was uncomfortable with her sense of self. Her self-esteem was low and she was constantly second guessing herself. This prevented her from creating positive first impressions and forming meaningful relationships until someone knew her for a very long time.

When her school mate met her at a party, the school mate was genuinely interested in what Mallika had to say. She praised Mallika on her work as a baker. Where Mallika saw herself as a failure, who did something on a very small scale, "nothing worth talking about", as she put it, things were different from her friend's view.

Here's what her friend had to say, "There are plenty of things to beat ourselves up with in the world. Let's at least start feeling good about the good things. You're doing well with the baking. You did it yourself. And that's an achievement in itself."

It wasn't that Mallika's view of herself changed all of a sudden. But it was the beginning of the road where she began coming out of her self-imposed negative view.

When do you know you have a blind side? When do you seek feedback?

Seeking feedback is a continuous affair. People constantly give you feedback through verbal, vocal and visual cues. Being receptive to it is the key. It is certainly time to seek active feedback under the following circumstances:

- When the same bad things continue to happen to you, as in Kaahini's case, when she continuously gets rejected in her interviews, or in Vineeta's case, when she continues to have a poor relationship with her teammates.
- When your luck never seems to hold.
- When you continuously make poor choices in partners, friends, bosses or work places.
- When people continuously turn their back to you during social occasions.
- When what people tell you does not meet your image of yourself, as in Mallika's case, when the friend's positive view was contrary to her own negative self-image.

These are just a few situations when feedback is necessary to bring your blind side into your view. When any situation happens repeatedly with many people, it is time to seek feedback.

Self-assessment and introspection are other necessary ways to arrive at the answer. Yet another way to keep the blind side to the minimum is to be open to new experiences and people, by going into these situations without preconceived notions.

The question is, how do you take negative feedback? It is one of the toughest things to do.

Just as Vineeta had done, don't contradict the person giving the feedback. You are not at the session to defend yourself, but to listen. You are there to see yourself from the other person's eyes. See that image as neutrally as you can. Don't add your interpretation as to what the person's intention was. Don't subtract from the feedback by dropping some points because they are uncomfortable. If necessary, seek clarifications. Giving or taking feedback requires an acceptance of others and of yourself. It requires self-mastery.

What do you do with this feedback?

What you now need to do is see if this feedback is valid. Run it through your filters. Discard feedback that is judgmental rather than evaluative. For example, "You can never do anything well" is judgmental. Ask for specific instances when such feedback comes. Take feedback which tells you what the other person feels and the concrete things which you can act upon such as, "I feel uncomfortable and stifled because you tend to micro-manage me."

The next step is to watch yourself in the actual situation, how you think, feel, and act. Changing the way you think in that situation, the way you feel and act requires you to watch yourself. It is what you need to do continuously to minimize your blind side.

3. WHO YOU COULD BE

Many people look at their past, or they look at their current situation and decide with disappointment that this is their reality forever. But, that is not necessarily true.

As Ralph Waldo Emerson said, "The only person you are destined to become is the person you decide to be."

What you have been was in the past. What you are today will soon be the past, too. What you will become is a matter of what you choose to become. This is the basic premise of first impressions.

Most of us have some idea of who we could be but choose to ignore that future part of us. This is the part that is critical to creating first impressions. Who you could be is a matter of who you dream of becoming, and how hard and how intelligently you work towards it.

Sally was in the running for a cooking competition. The mother of three, she and her husband had long discussions on whether she should enter the competition. Sally had always been a good cook, experimenting with dishes. She was particularly adept at desserts. Finally, knowing that cooking was important to her, her husband said he would take care of the family while she went away.

Surrounded by contestants, some half her age, many not married, and most with no children, took a lot of belief in her potential for her to even try out for the competition. What kept her going was her desire to be there.

Throughout the competition, she maximized every lesson taught and every opportunity she had. When everyone went back tired, they lazed over dinner or in bed. But, Sally cooked again and again, using the lessons and tips she learned that day until she perfected it. Through the three months of the competition, she improved by leaps and bounds. No surprise then, that she emerged the winner with the large prize money, a book deal and the chance to work with the nation's best chefs to further her learning.

Each of the contestants was as good as or better than Sally when they entered the competition. But, when it came to viewing their potential, no one could see it as clearly as Sally could. It wasn't that Sally thought she was already good enough to be there on the winner's stand. It was that she saw herself there and in seeing herself there, she also saw the path she had to take and worked at it diligently each day, even long after she was tired.

So, see yourself there, on that podium, and work towards it. That is your potential, your future self that is unknown to you.

Like Sally, we sometimes know what we want. What remains is to work for it. There are times, however, when all that points you toward that dream is dissatisfaction with the current situation or environment. With nothing more than this dissatisfaction as the starting point, it is probably time to look around, to take the risk, try out new things until you find a way that is more suitable than the beaten path. We don't know the goal. Others don't know it either. Life carries us along, but if we are unhappy doing what we do, it's time to explore.

Ravi was working towards his Bachelor's Degree in Science and he knew he wasn't happy doing it. His father knew he wasn't happy. Knowing that Ravi had some interest in art, his father brought in brochures of fine arts colleges across the country. They pored over the brochures and then decided that the best way to know was to go visit some of them.

Said Ravi, "We went to the Fine Arts College in Baroda. I stepped into a studio and in that instant, I knew. I knew that this was what I wanted to do." Ravi is now a fine painter and head of the department in a reputed arts studio.

What about now? How do I influence first impressions to reach where I want to reach?

Let's suppose you are attending an interview for the position of a general manager. This would be an elevation from your current level of senior manager. How do you project yourself in such a situation?

You imagine yourself in the position of the general manager and you think, speak and act like one. The person interviewing you wants to see you as the general manager, not merely as someone with the potential to become a general manager. How you behave influences what you think. So when you behave like the general manager you want to be, you automatically begin to feel like a general manager and this in turn reinforces the behaviour. This positive cycle of reinforcement influences you and the stranger.

In conclusion, many of us have issues with our image. But, the more self-aware you are, the better equipped you are at controlling what you show. Working with self-mastery raises your ability to take feedback and in your self-disclosure. Forgive yourself. It is an important factor in building self-esteem. Carry a positive mental attitude. Correct self-defeating behaviour — clothe and groom yourself right, make eye contact, walk with ease, carry a body language that speaks of your inner confidence. Seek positive experiences. Build the skills — communication and social skills.

The day you enter the room with the confidence that speaks louder than words, "I am worthwhile," is the day you have achieved the self that can create positive first impressions each time, every time.

REFERENCES

1 http://acquirewisdom.blogspot.com/2007/04/know-yourself-well.html

2 http://business.nmsu.edu/~dboje/503/johari_window.htm

SO FAR

- Creating a positive first impression in the stranger's mind is in your hands.
- Self-awareness gives you the capacity to learn from your mistakes as well as your successes.
- Recognize the labels you give yourself and those that the world gives you.
- Make a conscious effort to project your strengths.
- The Cycle of Image Projection relies on five factors:
  - Self-awareness
  - Self-disclosure
  - Incorporating feedback into self-awareness and self-disclosure
  - Self-esteem and
  - Self-mastery which along with self-esteem creates a positive cycle of image projection.
- Self-esteem without self-mastery can lead to arrogance and pride.
- The question 'Who Am I' comprises three parts:
  - Who you are (Which you know) — Disclose the positives and minimize the negatives
  - Who you are (Which you don't know) — Know your blind side through feedback and self-mastery
  - Who you could be — Project an image appropriate to the position that you decide to reach.

Chapter 9

How the World Sees You

Whatever I see something as, depending on my perception of it, that's what it will be to me.

— Anonymous

Nirav was a business consultant to a client company in Ahmedabad. When he flew down from Delhi to spend the day meeting the new business head of the company's real estate division, he began on a negative note.

Nirav's shirt was rumpled as if he had been in it a whole day, his hair ruffled and untidy. He compounded the negative image when he opened the conversation, complaining about his delayed start to the day, "I can't believe the amount of time they made us sit in the aircraft waiting for clearance. We boarded at 6 am and then waited for two hours. I'd been up most of the night, preparing for the trip which made the waiting even more difficult. When we finally landed, I couldn't find the cab that was to bring me to the office. By the time I picked another and reached the office, it felt as if a day had gone by."

Nirav was just giving vent to his feelings. Afterall, they were fresh in his mind, but they were negative and the business head was taken by surprise.

With that beginning, despite the fact that Nirav was well-prepared for the meeting and that the company representatives treated him with respect, the business head formed a negative impression of Nirav. No amount of focus and diligence from Nirav could change this. After that, the business head found it hard to relate to Nirav.

Maybe you've had a bad day like Nirav did. Maybe things beyond your control have forced you to arrive late, flustered and stressed. Maybe it's just the way you look at things — that things always go wrong for you. But, they leave a negative first impression.

Warmth and competency, according to Professor Amy Cuddy of Harvard Business School, are what people look for when they form first impressions. Basically, they are answering the very important questions of — Are you good for me? Or, are you bad for me? In social life, are your intentions toward me good? In business life, will your efforts for me be effective? Nirav's image on arrival at the client's office didn't meet the warmth and competency parameters that the business head was likely looking for.

Plenty of times we, too, rush into a meeting a few minutes late because things are seemingly out of our control. In our rush to make up for it, we compound the negative start by trying to explain what went wrong or begin the meeting abruptly, all of which leaves a negative impression on people.

Why don't strangers understand that there was an external reason for these actions? How do strangers form their first impressions? How do they come to the judgment of whether you are good for them? What is the basis of their judgment?

Strangers are not forming first impressions in a vacuum, where they look at each person afresh. If that were so, they would be reasoning logically before they form a first impression. On the contrary, they form intuitive, rapid impressions. In doing so, they are bringing into play their knowledge and experience of similar persons and situations.

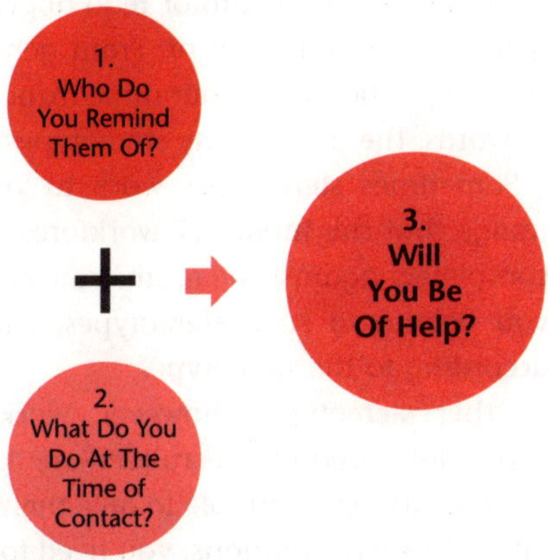

This explains why preschoolers were found to use more analytical thinking skills than stereotyping that comes from experience and knowledge. They simply haven't lived long enough to build the required stereotypes. When the preschoolers became familiar with the stereotypes, their performance began to be affected[1].

While it is understood that the more people gain in knowledge and experience as they grow, the more their first impressions are based on rapid, intuitive judgments. In reality, three factors affect their judgments.

1. Who do you remind them of?
2. What do you do at the time of contact?
3. Will you be of help?

The first impressions that you create are the sum total of the person's knowledge and experience of people, groups and situations and what you are doing at the moment when they set their eyes on you. They use this information to decide whether you are likely to fulfill their goals. In those few seconds, all that information reflects on you and your image is fixed in their mind.

1. Who Do You Remind Them of?

Every time you step into a room full of strangers, say hello or to shake hands with a stranger, you are being stereotyped. To make judgements about you, people rely on stereotypes of those they have met earlier, heard or read about. A stereotype is an image of who you remind them of. From gender to cultural stereotypes, to stereotypes based on your appearance, posture, diction, and choice of words, there are many stereotypes to relate to.

Sometimes stereotypes work to your advantage, like the tech image that the Indian IT workforce carries abroad. Unless you go completely against the grain, you start off on a positive note when you belong to such stereotypes. All you have to do is behave according to the stereotype.

Other stereotypes, however, work to your disadvantage. For example, corporate recruiters are known to stereotype working mothers as being unable to give their complete focus to work at an office. In such situations, you need to bring all the elements of first impressions — clothing, grooming, body language, including etiquette and vocal communication into play to prove that you are the exception to such stereotypes.

How do stereotypes operate?

Stereotypes emerge from the fact that we have two different thinking and decision-making modes, as discussed in Chapter—1 What are First Impressions?

- The intuitive method, which happens automatically. This relies on pre-existing knowledge and experience to extrapolate from the few facts they have about you.
- The logical method, which is analytical. This is based on reasoning and takes time because it takes into consideration all the facts necessary. It is demanding and burdens our working memory.

According to research by Professor Wim De Neys, intuitive thinking based on stereotypes is too tempting for our brains to use, as compared to laborious logical thinking. For an experiment in which a room was supposedly filled with 995 lawyers and 5 engineers, people had to answer the question, "Who might the person be if he is 45 years old, has four children, little interest in political or social issues, is generally conservative, likes sailing and mathematical puzzles?"

The brain's stereotype detector lit up irrespective of whether the people answered stereotypically, that it is an engineer or logically, that it is a lawyer. With just 5 engineers in the room, the chances of the person being a lawyer were the highest. But, the logical part lit up only when they reasoned that the person was a lawyer[2]. Stereotypes kick in automatically and it takes conscious effort to override what the stereotype is telling us.

Why do people stereotype?

Stereotypes make it easier and faster for people to make their decisions. They are a carryover from our ancestors' jungle survival kit. For example, the alpha wolf in a pack of wolves makes a quick decision not to allow a strange wolf into his pack since it could be a threat. Similarly, people make quick decisions in determining whether or not you belong to their tribe. Essentially, the stranger is judging quickly whether you are a friend or a foe, and whether or not they can have a future relationship with you. But to form this quick decision, the stranger needs more information up front. There are still gaps in the information you offer in the first few seconds. Given this scenario, what does the stranger do? They fill in the gaps based on stereotypes.

They bring all their knowledge and experience, which they have learned from others through the media and their own life experiences, to the judgment table. They look inward to see who you remind him of. They extrapolate from the few visual, olfactory and vocal cues that you display. They fill in the gaps in the information by coming to a quick conclusion about who you remind them of. They file you into that stereotype in their mind. Their first impression is formed.

Yet, no two persons see the same information and process it in exactly the same way. The way they fill the gaps differs based on the person and the situation. This complicates the way stereotypes work.

How do stereotypes work? How does it affect you?

All of us belong to multiple groups or tribes. People associate certain stereotypes with these tribes. Common stereotypes are based on culture or race, gender, age, religion, language, country, the state or region within a country, community, preferences, education, work sphere and more.

Take for example, the time when I was driving around a large traffic circle and was forced to stop suddenly. Right in the middle of the road were a couple of young men in their late teens or early twenties sitting on a bike.

It looked to me like the rider had a cell phone in his left hand. I honked and I honked, assuming in that split second that while his bike may have stopped in the middle of the road, instead of pulling it aside, he chose to take a call.

My assumption was based on the many times I had seen people talking on cell phones while they blocked the road for others. I had also seen youngsters flouting traffic rules defiantly.

Finally, when the boy moved his bike, I realized to my great shame that he didn't have a cell phone in his hand. His bike had stalled and as geared two-wheelers sometimes do, it wouldn't budge. There wasn't time to apologize, we went around the traffic circle with other cars behind us and I moved on.

What went wrong? Why did I form those instant impressions? Bike in the middle of the road, youth, partially hidden left hand — that's all my brain had time to process. Irritation coursed through my body and I reacted. The stereotype had influenced my judgment.

How do I manage such stereotypes? How can I take advantage of the stereotype that the stranger wants to see? Or, how can I make stereotypes work to my advantage?

With little time to respond, countering stereotypes requires preparation and an awareness of the stereotypes involved.

Situations like the traffic circle and the halted bike, where the incident is sudden and is over within seconds, are rare and you literally have no time to think about your reaction. But in most situations, self-awareness and self-mastery can give you an understanding of the tribes involved and the expected stereotype. Since the stranger comes with a huge body of knowledge and experience, countering the stereotype effectively also requires knowledge of the stereotypes that apply to you.

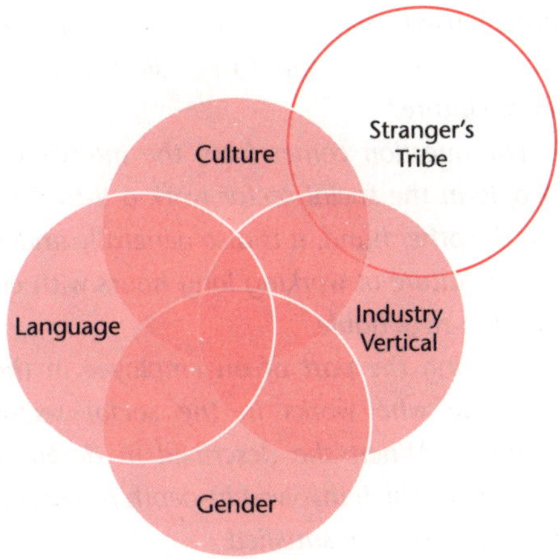

Your Tribes Vs Stranger's Tribes

In the image (on the right), the tribes that you belong to are only representative. In reality, there are many more. What is important is the fact that the stranger's tribes sometimes overlap with yours. You need to begin with them as the common point, reinforcing the fact that you belong to those tribes, by making effective use of the elements of first impressions, namely, clothing, grooming, body language, including etiquette and vocal communication. This helps you neutralize the impact of belonging to an unrelated tribe, by projecting your membership in the tribe that you share with the stranger. Finding this common ground is the way to gain entry into the stranger's world. By showing this aspect of yourself, you have fulfilled the stranger's stereotype and have fit into his world, which is just what the stranger seeks.

Sheela was applying for the job as a senior writer in a financial services company. Coming from her current job in the social sector, which dealt with consumer complaints and legal issues in the banking and insurance domains, Sheela anticipated questions related to her work culture.

She was well prepared to project a positive first impression. She dressed in formal clothing that included black trousers, a cream coloured shirt and black shoes. The only pieces of jewellery she wore were a thin leather-strapped watch and tiny pearl stud earrings.

It didn't take long for the anticipated question to be raised, "Having gotten used to the work culture of an organization involved in social work, will you be able to handle the demands of the financial services work culture?"

The question comes from the interviewer's assumed stereotype, that people in the social sector work a 9-to-5 job with negotiable deadlines. On the other hand, it is also generally understood that the finance sector has a culture of working long hours with customer-driven timelines that are non-negotiable.

Dressing the part of an employee in the finance sector rather than someone who works in the social sector gave support to Sheela's response. When she described in detail research documents she had prepared, which involved in-depth research, analysis and long hours, the interviewers were satisfied.

When facing situations in the business, social or personal life, it helps to put yourself in the stranger's shoes. To successfully understand the stereotypes you are labelled with, you require self-awareness. Not just of the individual self, but also of the tribes you belong to. The next step is to understand the tribe the stranger is likely to belong to. Contrast the two tribes and learn the differences. Also, learn the perceptions, habits, conversations, clothing, grooming, body language, etiquette and vocal habits of each of the tribes. Make a conscious effort to disclose the traits that you have in common with the stranger.

Long before she entered the interview room, Sheela had a professional person review her resume and make suggestions so that it met the expectations of the finance sector. As a member of the legal department at her current workplace, she had handled many cases which were financial and legal in nature. She highlighted this experience in her resume.

As we had seen earlier, she had taken care to dress appropriately in western formals for the interview hoping to prevent any further association with the work culture of the social sector. Finally, she prepared well for the anticipated questions by finding common work areas with the financial sector.

In the example above, Sheela projected herself as part of the finance sector through her clothing and communication, conveying effectively the message that she can belong to the financial services sector. This is particularly critical when the stranger does not ask questions during the meeting or interview to confirm his impression of the stereotype you belong to.

How do I know when I will be unable to overcome a stereotype?
When the stranger does not change his view despite repeated information that contradicts the stereotype, it has become a prejudice, a deep seated belief that they are unwilling to change. You cannot overcome a prejudice with the limited time at your disposal. You may as well accept it and move on with your task at hand.

A more innocent explanation for a fixed stereotype is when the stranger is in a negative mood, is tired or stressed out. According to Dr. Nalini Ambady, people who were induced into a happy mood by watching a scene from a happy movie were more accurate in their prediction of a teacher's effectiveness from a video clip than those who were induced into a sad mood[3]. When people are tired or stressed, they have little mental energy or focus to go past generalizations, unless you appear to be in such complete contrast to the stereotype that they cannot ignore you.

While you may have no control over the person's mood, it is in your best interest to have important meetings scheduled at a more reasonable hour and not in the thick of things, if that is possible. You can then be reasonably sure that the person is able to focus on you.

2. What do You do at the Time of Contact?

What you look like and what you do at the point of contact have an overriding effect on first impressions. Your clothing, grooming, body language, including etiquette and vocal communication, all come into play. The stranger takes them in at a glance and forms first impressions.

Is that all there is to it? All I have to do is look and behave appropriately?

Well, yes, you do have to look and behave in a manner that projects the appropriate image. Based on the image you project through the four elements the stranger's mind forms an impression of your personality.

In Nirav's case, the business head concluded that the rumpled attire and grooming indicated a lack of professionalism on Nirav's part. Further, the complaints in the opening conversation pointed to a similar outlook in life. This led to a negative first impression and the business head did not appreciate Nirav. It didn't seem to matter that the company's employees held Nirav in high regard, based on his focus, insights and professionalism and found him an easy peer to work with.

Studies show that when it comes to ourselves, we attribute external factors to our failure and internal factors to our success. On the other hand, when it comes to judging others, we tend to attribute internal factors to their failure or wrongdoing and external factors to their success[4]. The business head had done just that when it came to judging Nirav.

Similarly, people often have their expectations for different situations and then look for cues that meet these expectations. A slice of you and your behaviour at that point in time is taken as representative of you. An extrapolation is made to form impressions of your personality. Your behaviour at that point in time may be a one-of-a-kind behaviour arising out of a specific situation. That becomes irrelevant when it comes to first impressions. They have seen a reality which you have displayed knowingly or unknowingly.

Imagine walking into a party in full swing when you see a boisterous man who has had more than his share of drinks. What is your first impression? You are likely to perceive it as irresponsible behaviour and attribute it to his entire personality. You have given precedence to the inner factors and you take him off your list of potentially enduring relationships. Before the person even sees you or an introduction is made, a lasting negative impression is formed in your mind.

In reality, it is possible that he is celebrating a good day in the middle of stressful times, or trying to mitigate the pain of a very bad day or maybe his drinks were mixed without his knowledge.

Although formal occasions offer us the chance to be prepared for the occasion, we do slip up like Nirav did when we speak about what is fresh on our mind. Preventing such negative occurrences from affecting us and continuing in a positive frame of mind is essential to creating positive first impressions. After all, since one of the factors that people are looking for is warmth, a positive outlook in life meets this requirement. Temporary factors should not overshadow your permanent self.

When it comes to informal social occasions, however free the atmosphere might look, your clothing, grooming, body language including etiquette and vocal communication need to be appropriate for the occasion. This is particularly necessary where your social life overlaps with your business life and expectations could conflict. In the case of official social gatherings or social gatherings where you expect to build business relations, the ideal approach is to take a semi-business approach and balance the formal with just a slightly casual behaviour and dressing.

Remember, your actions speak louder than words.

3. Will You be of Help?

The underlying goal, across the board, is in forming relationships. Building on this foundation are different concrete goals. When you meet strangers in your business, social, personal and public lives, they are constantly asking themselves, "Can I or my company build a relationship with this person?"

These goals and the type of potential relationship depend on the situation, the third component in first impressions alongside you and the stranger. Every first impression is based on a situation where the stranger is trying to maximize benefit to himself or his company while minimizing pain. Hence, they come with certain goals and expectations, just as you project a certain image based on your situation.

The question is, how do you know what the stranger's goal is? Some situations are highly formal with clearly defined goals. For example, business situations have goals like hiring the right candidate or gaining the contract. Certain personal situations have goals that focus on selecting a potential spouse or meeting family members to gain their approval and so on. Here, the goals are clear and known to both sides although the preparation can be quite lengthy.

In each of these cases, the underlying goal continues to be one of forming healthy, long-term relationships. For example, when a business situation is centered on hiring a candidate, the interviewer's goal is to see if they or their company can form a business relationship with the candidate.

Other situations have no concrete goal, but may have peripheral or associated goals. For example, you have started college where the primary purpose is to learn. The associated goals are to make friends and form groups that help you perform your tasks effectively and act as a support system. Although in this case, there are no concrete relationship goals, forming relationships with others does take center stage.

What do strangers seek in these different lives?

According to research by Professor Amy Cuddy at the Harvard Business School and psychologists Susan Fiske and Peter Glick, people judge others for warmth and competence. While warmth denotes their friendly intentions, competence refers to their ability to deliver on those intentions[5]. Warmth without competence elicits pity. Competence without warmth brings out envy and aggression. In isolation, neither results in positive first impressions.

In business situations, the stranger looks for competence, integrity and commitment in you. In personal lives, warmth, commitment, integrity and a shared outlook on life could be the goal. Given that your business and personal lives overlap with your social life, you might be forming potential acquaintances and business relationships or you might be forming friendships, meeting a potential spouse or family member. Hence, each of the aspects that the stranger seeks in your business and personal lives — warmth, competence, integrity and commitment — come into play with varying degrees of importance depending on your goal.

All of us are familiar with the fact that we dress and behave differently for different situations. Similarly, the stranger's judgment depends on the situation. The good thing about the influence of the situation is that it gives you important cues as to the stranger's expectations.

In our earlier example, Sheela had an interview in the financial services sector for the profile of a writer. She knew that once she got past their stereotypes, she had a good chance of being selected. She had taken extra care with her resume, her looks, clothing and communication to display that she belonged to the financial sector.

A little thought and preparation prior to the interview helped her meet the interviewer's expectations.

Similarly, when you know that the business dinner is meant to be an exercise in relationship-building, you know that it is a semi-formal affair. You dress accordingly in evening wear that suits business dinners rather than a social dinner.

With each situation, the stranger's expectations differ. Preparing with the situation in mind helps you dress and groom yourself appropriately for the occasion.

Sometimes, the situation is beyond your control. How do you respond in such cases?

Where the situation is beyond your control, the stranger does not have the time to consider the reason. It is for you to choose your response. Two scenarios need discussion here. One is where the negative situation controls your emotions. The second is where you let the negative situation determine the path for you.

In Nirav's case when things were beyond his control and his day started on a bad note, it was necessary to accept that things don't go as expected and that negative things can happen at the worst possible moment. It is your response to those occasions that shows up as your real self, in short, your ability to control your emotions.

Self-mastery is crucial here. When bad things happen, some view the world with a negative outlook, "Nothing good happens to me," and their entire demeanour reflects that. Unfortunately, for them, the world holds up a mirror to them and they receive what they give — a negative impression. But, others continue to carry a positive outlook. They have the emotional intelligence and the self-mastery to say, "This is a bad situation that can happen to anyone. I will get on with my day."

Many of us fall between these two extremes. We carry the negative outlook for a short period, letting it go eventually. The need is to let it go fast and this requires self-mastery.

Other times, negative situations determine the path for you. In such cases, you need to set your priorities right. Sometimes, driven by the stress of overlapping work and time factors, we allow our options to be chosen by these stress factors without giving a thought as to what we really want to do.

Prominent social psychologists John M.Darley and C.Daniel Batson decided to test the parable of the Good Samaritan from the Bible. The parable is of a Jewish man travelling to Jericho. Bandits attack the man and leave him half-dead by the road. A priest and temple assistant walk past without offering help. On the other hand, a Good Samaritan, who stereotypically hated Jews, offered assistance.

After being told this parable, when students were tested, a greater percentage of students were found to offer help to a man in distress when they were not stressed for time. In this research example, the time factor affected the student behaviour[6]*.*

Each time you allow a stress factor or a negative emotion to determine your path or emotion, you are inviting potentially negative first impressions. There is no easy solution to overcoming this. It lies in working towards self-mastery so that you retain a balanced outlook and have your priorities in order.

But none of the stranger's decisions are in my hands, some say. How can I influence what the other person thinks, particularly when all I have is a few seconds at the most?

What is within your control is to understand the stranger's belief system and project your image with accuracy and credibility. To do so, you need to know the person in front of you, what she sees in you and what kind of first impression she is likely to form of you.

Without this world view, we think in isolation. Considering that we live in a society where our business, social, personal, intimate and public lives intersect with that of hundreds of people's lives, such isolation can be disastrous.

It takes self-awareness and self-mastery discussed in Chapter 8 to be able to place yourself in others' shoes, capture their perceptions and project your image with credibility.

What if the stranger's expectations do not match what I currently am?

While it is true that projecting your inner self is the authentic way to creating positive first impressions, there are occasions when this self is not credible for the stranger — it does not meet the stranger's goals.

In such cases, we can influence how we feel and our inner self by acting the image we would like to project. According to Professor Amy Cuddy, when we put on the body posture that conveys, for example, competence and power for as little as two minutes, it changes our testosterone and cortisol levels. The power poses used in her study were first, the classic feet on desk, hands behind head; then, standing and leaning on one's hands over a desk. She found that such poses increase our appetite for risk, cause us to perform better in job interviews and help our brain to cope well in stressful situations. If you act the image that you want to project, you begin to think the same way[7].

Being authentic and credible is what you are trying to achieve, says author and academic, Dr. Laura Morgan Roberts[8].

"It's like wanting to have the cake and eat it too," said Amit. He was referring to the struggle in creating first impressions that are true to himself while having an impact on others.

As Dr.Roberts says, remaining authentic to your true self and building credibility with others are crucial to forming positive impressions. Your true self may not always meet the stranger's goals and expectations. Building this credibility means being what others want you to be. But if you suppress your identity to meet this credibility, you may receive some short-term benefits, but it does not work in the long-term. So, when you project a self that is not true to you, work towards building that self only if that is your objective.

How does your view of the world affect the image you project and the impressions you create? How can you convert a negative situation into a positive one?

Some are negative situations that begin on a bad note, either due to stereotypes that are unfavourable to you, or due to your behaviour or conflicting goals. Some are negative situations because of your world view. As author Anais Nin has said, "We don't see things as they are, we see things as we are." Those who see the world as a negative place, face negative situations. Those who view the world with a positive outlook, find it a positive place that aims to do good to them.

In either case, preparation and self-mastery hold the key to converting a negative situation into a positive one. Being at the receiving end of a negative stereotype is a frustrating, anxiety-ridden situation that gets our stress levels up. Our immediate reaction is to respond in kind. When faced with an abrasive or aggressive individual, we tend to respond instinctively with the same abrasiveness or other tactics like stonewalling.

Our mood has a lot to do with the first impressions we wish to create. How do we respond to an indifferent waiter, a rude colleague, or the security guard at the mall who wants to check our purchases? Responding in kind merely escalates the situation and is of no benefit to you except the short-term benefit of relieving your anger. Staying calm and responding with patience as if the stereotyping did not occur defuses the situation and turns a negative situation into a more positive one.

Your self-mastery, the emotional intelligence you carry, helps you regulate your emotions and place yourself in the other person's shoes — a tough thing to do in highly charged situations. But, you can build this self-mastery with time and effort.

The way we look at ourselves determines how we see the world. In turn, the way we see the world impacts how we see ourselves. You can treat this as a vicious circle that continually drags you down or you can make it a circle of escalating success. You can be the creator of your own first impressions.

In conclusion, it helps to look at yourself, the strangers you face, their requirements and the situation. This gives you important clues for how to create a powerful, positive first impression. You may not have control over how the stranger sees you, but if you know where the stranger is coming from, you can influence how you project yourself. That is the art and science of creating powerful positive first impressions.

REFERENCES

1 http://www.wdeneys.org/data/preprint_online.pdf

2 http://www.psychologicalscience.org/onlyhuman/2008/04/neurology-of-stereotypes_24.cfm

3 http://www.apa.org/monitor/mar05/slices.aspx

4 Social Psychology and Human Nature, by Roy F.Baumeister, Brad J.Bushman

5 http://www.scientificamerican.com/article.cfm?id=mixed-impressions

6 "From Jerusalem to Jericho": A study of situational and dispositional variables in helping behaviour, http://faculty.babson.edu/krollag/org_site/soc_psych/darley_samarit.html

7 http://www.tedxcambridge.com/thrive/amy-cuddy/ and http://hbswk.hbs.edu/item/6461.html

8 http://hbswk.hbs.edu/item/4860.html

SO FAR

- Strangers form intuitive, rapid impressions when they meet you the first time, based on their knowledge and experience.
- Three factors affect these rapid impressions:
    - Who do you remind them of?
    - What do you do at the time of contact?
    - Will you be of help?
- Make the stereotype work to your advantage.
- Some common stereotypes are of culture, race, gender, age, religion, language, country, state, community, preferences, education, work sphere.
- People accept individual exceptions to their beliefs of a particular stereotype.
- Stereotypes can be overcome, but not prejudices.
- Find common tribes with the stranger to build a relationship on.
- You would attribute external factors to your failure, but strangers attribute internal factors to your failure.
- Strangers are unlikely to see the reason behind your temporary negative behaviour, but make inferences about your personality.
- People's expectations for different situations make them look for cues from you that meet these expectations.
- The stranger forms a relationship with you based on whether you are likely to meet his objectives.
- In business life, people look for competence, integrity and commitment.
- In personal life, they look for warmth, competence, integrity and a shared outlook.
- Self-awareness and self-mastery help you project the right image regardless of the situation and expectations.

Chapter 10

Correcting Negative First Impressions

A poor choice of words conveyed to some the impression that I embrace the discarded policies of the past. Nothing could be further from the truth, and I apologize to anyone who was offended by my statement.

— Trent Lott, former United States Senator

Nalin had just walked out of an interview with the Vice-President — Human Resources of a well-known textile company. With over 10 years of experience behind him, Nalin should have been quite comfortable at the interview. But, it was one of the largest companies in the field and the stakes were high. Putting on more pressure was the fact that the Vice-President chose to conduct the interview. Nalin felt out of place and was restricted in his responses, answering to the point and without elaboration as he should.

The Vice-President was trying to gauge Nalin's capabilities as a middle manager, operational excellence and a strategic outlook. Despite repeated probing, Nalin's inability to provide sufficiently elaborate responses that addressed the concerns resulted in a weak first impression. Consequently, the Vice-President decided to reject Nalin as a candidate.

Nalin knew it even as he stepped out of the interview. Luckily for him, his flight was delayed and he made other arrangements while in the lobby. He also had the time to think through what had happened in the interview, and he knew he had not performed well. The Vice-President happened to walk out at the same time and decided to have lunch with Nalin. Fact was, Nalin's resume looked too good for the actual person not to have met his expectations.

They sat for lunch in the cafeteria where Nalin relaxed. With that, conversation was no longer formal, and they had a good chat. Nalin was able to explain things better. The happy result was that the Vice-President decided to clear his interview with the unit head. Nalin was selected and went on to do well in the company.

Making powerful positive first impressions has great impact on our business, social and personal lives. Each of us wants to make great first impressions. Unfortunately, we don't always do that.

Maybe you forgot to respond to an email or phone call when it was expected. Maybe you were late for an appointment because of heavy traffic or a prior meeting. Maybe you had sent an inappropriate e-mail to the wrong person. Maybe you got into a heated argument at a social or family occasion. Maybe you had committed a social faux pas, did not remember a person's name or your humour was out of place. Maybe it was just a temporary negative mood that made you give a negative response, leaving a poor first impression.

While most of us may not have such second chances in interviews, you may have opportunities on other occasions. If you are quick about assessing the situation, you can even turn the interview around.

Although getting a second opportunity like Nalin did is pure chance, the incident did happen. Nalin had time to collect himself, assess his performance and realize where he had gone wrong. The lunch was an unforeseen opportunity which he was able to utilize to reverse the original weak first impression. To help matters, the second occasion was informal enough for him to relax.

While first impressions become lasting impressions, there is much that you can do to change the impression. The sooner you begin to make an active effort to change the weak or negative impression, the better the results are. As we shall explain later in this chapter, sometimes, your effort begins even before the impression is formed.

It is true that first impressions are lasting impressions. But not all is lost. There is a chance that you can change the first impression, although it is not an easy task.

Once the stranger has formed his impression, anything that runs counter to it may be ignored. Changing this involves changing his perceptions which had led to the impression in the first place. Later experiences may correct previous impressions. With consistent effort, you may modifiy that earlier Impression. Recognize that there are times when any effort from you may only make the first impression worse.

We shall discuss these scenarios and what you must do in each case in this chapter.

1. How to change a negative first impression.
2. When to ignore the negative first impression.
3. Creating positive lasting impressions.

The important thing in any of these scenarios is to project the real you. When you project a different image, it remains a short-term achievement. In the long-term, people have more time to read you and when the real image emerges, you will be perceived as insincere. This is worse than leaving a poor first impression, losing their respect and trust. Retaining your sense of self and projecting the real you requires self-mastery and self-esteem.

1. How to Change a Negative First Impression

It is important for you to try and improve on most negative impressions. With repercussions ranging from not getting the job you wanted, from not getting the raise you felt you deserve, from strained family relationships or from finding yourself at the periphery of the social life around you, they leave a deep impact on your life.

What you do subsequent to the negative impression and how soon you do it have great impact on future impressions. Some fairly universal rules apply to correcting negative first impressions. They are based on what had gone wrong by saying the wrong words, doing the wrong thing or having conflicting tribes or traits.

RETAIN A POSITIVE ATTITUDE

The warmth, commitment and efficiency that people look for in a stranger are projected by your positive attitude and positive words. These are at the core of forming a relationship. When you complain, speak negatively of a third person, pose intrusive questions, argue your point aggressively or get into a personal attack, you are displaying a negative attitude. To the stranger, these indicate a lack of warmth and commitment to others. When you give excuses for not meeting a promise, you display a lack of commitment and efficiency.

The solution to the negative impressions created by these words lies in the problem itself.

- Retain a positive attitude. This comes with self-esteem and self-mastery.
- Do not let a temporary adversity affect your mood, forcing you to say words you would regret later. Don't be negative in your conversations. Even if you are frustrated due to a temporary bad experience, take a deep breath and consciously strive to convey a positive attitude.
- Count to 10 before you respond when you find yourself on the verge of giving a negative response. This will help you cool down and give a more neutral response.
- Do not criticize. Negative words that serve no purpose are best left unsaid. When you are asked to give your honest opinion

and if it happens to be a negative opinion, think before you speak. Then change your response. In your personal and social lives where it is simply a matter of conversation, you do not have to reveal your negative opinions. Apart from the fact that word has a way of getting around, people respect you for your good words. In business situations where it becomes necessary, use neutral words, don't ascribe negative adjectives when giving your opinion. Give reasons for your opinion.

- When your opinion is contrary to the popular one or that of the stranger's, state your view neutrally and calmly. Remember, you need to be truthful. If a heated discussion takes place, don't get aggressive and attack the other's view point and definitely don't attack the person. If the discussion continues, don't give in to the urge to agree to the stranger's view point just to prevent an escalation. The stranger may not like your viewpoint, but when you give in, you will be perceived as weak and lacking the strength to hold on to your opinion.
- Take responsibility for mistakes. Don't give excuses. Don't blame others.
- Don't apologize repeatedly. It will be seen as a weakness. After completing the apology, be your natural self and come to the business at hand. Remain positive and empathetic to the stranger.
- Use a different situation to project the right image. For example, even if the stranger has formed a poor impression of you during a social situation, he may be ready to accept a different impression in a business situation. This second impression will be limited to business situations. Use that as the beginning. Then over time, work towards expanding this image to other situations.

USE APPROPRIATE HUMOUR

Used well, humour can create a strong positive first impression. But if it is out of place it can leave behind a very negative first impression. Humour may be a great way of reaching out to people. But it often falls flat, or worse — it hurts someone. People perceive humour differently. Different cultures have different meanings to humour. What is humour to one culture may be offensive to another.

- When using humour, take care that it is appropriate to the occasion. When the stakes are high and when you are not sure, avoid it.
- Humour is best used against yourself or when it is based on incidents. Don't use it against a third person or the stranger himself. From being perceived as a personal attack or a group attack on their tribe, it can make people see you as prejudiced. It can hurt them too much for you to have a comeback.
- Don't make it so light that the stranger feels you haven't taken the situation or him seriously.

MEET YOUR COMMITMENTS

Whether breaking promises or not living up to promises, both acts leave you vulnerable to weak and negative first impressions. When it comes to expectations, people have stated and unstated expectations about you. While the former are quite clear, you need to be observant to come to know the latter.

George had at last been given an appointment to meet the Director — Research and Development of a pharmaceutical company regarding the purchase of equipment for their facility. The order could be a potentially large one for him, but he had miscalculated the time it would take to reach the company which was at a remote location about an hour's drive from the city. George had already crossed the city limits and was on his way when he realized that he would be delayed by almost half an hour.

In this case, George had broken his promise to be at the meeting on time, an unstated expectation. If we go back to the first example of this chapter where the Vice-President — Human Resources does not see Nalin's potential, it is a case of Nalin not living up to the Vice-President's expectations. These incidents leave a poor first impression.

This is true for a range of actions in the business context. They may involve arriving late for a meeting, not sending a promised e-mail, not completing a project report on time and more. In the personal and social lives, it can involve a failure to live up to promises made to the spouse, children, family members or friends.

In the rush of things, it is easy to tell ourselves that one tiny deviation does not matter. But it does.

In George's case, he immediately called the company. When he was put through to the Director-R&D, George conveyed the information that he would be late for the appointment and apologized for it. He also asked if the Director would like to reschedule the meeting to another day or time.

It had taken George three months of consistent follow-up over e-mails and phone calls to the purchase and R&D managers before he could secure the appointment with the Director.

Considering that the person he was meeting was the Director, one of the highest in rank and hence with a tight schedule, George fully expected him to change the date. To his surprise, the Director said he would switch his meetings, but that George may have to wait a half hour or more until the meeting concluded. George was happy to agree.

George did have to wait close to an hour, but when the meeting began, he thanked the Director for accommodating him, admitted that he had been wrong in his calculation of time and distance, apologized for the delay and understood that it affected the Director's busy schedule. With that he began his presentation.

George had worked with the purchase and R&D managers to map their requirements with his company's equipment. He understood their concern for longevity and ROI and factored them into his calculations.

The fact that he was fully prepared and the fact that he had worked extensively with the company's teams helped him know the potential questions and be prepared with answers.

A few questions required substantiation, and George promised to send these details the next day. One question involved rechecking some figures. He promised to do that and send it within 48 hours. He later made good on his promises.

As in George's case, the solution lay in what he did before, during and after the incident.

- Actions speak louder than words. Prepare well in advance for meetings, interviews and presentations. The delay, for example, cannot be the last in the line of errors you have committed. It can be the only one. This will help you catch up fast and present yourself well.
- Inform beforehand and ask for a rescheduling of tasks, timelines or other requirements based on the situation. By doing this and by leaving it to the Director to decide a change in timing, George has shown courtesy. He has also shown his perception that the Director's time is valuable. The result was that the Director responded positively.
- While you are at the meeting or within the situation, assess the situation, the stranger and your feelings continuously.
- Change your approach based on your assessment.
- Apologize immediately. The sooner the better.
- Once the meeting is over, make sure that you meet your other promises whether they include rechecking certain facts or sharing some files or figures. Any delay or deviation at this point will only reinforce the weak first impression.
- Meet the promises consistently in the future. It takes many future impressions to change the perception of a first impression.

Is there a way to apologize effectively?

Apologizing effectively is more than a simple 'sorry'. There are five components to it — the apology itself, your reason for the wrong act, how it affects the others, the future course of action and the consistency with which you meet expectations and promises in future.

Firstly, the apology must be relevant and balanced. It can be neither too little nor excessive. Nor can it be too late. George was late for the meeting. Without giving excuses for his delay, he apologized immediately.

Secondly, give the reason behind not meeting your promise. Make sure that it is not an excuse. An excuse places the blame elsewhere. A reason makes you take responsibility for the incident and helps people empathize with you. An apology without reason does not help much. You do not have to go extensively into the reasons, some of which might be personal, but a touch of humour directed at yourself or at the situation can help.

Thirdly, acknowledge how the others are affected. Giving the reason is just your half of the story. Acknowledging the other's pain completes the other half. That is when you stand a chance of changing the initial poor image.

Fourthly, move on to the task at hand almost as if the earlier incident had not happened. Retaining that incident in your mind is a sure way of carrying a negative feeling within yourself. If you start off on the wrong foot mentally, you are likely to create the same image you had in the first place. Remember what we said in Chapter 9, Know the World, be the image you want to be in the first place and you will end up creating the same image in your mind and you will be more likely to live that image. Make a clean break and continue with a positive attitude. In doing so, you are helping the stranger think like you do, that it was an isolated incident caused by the situation and is not characteristic of you.

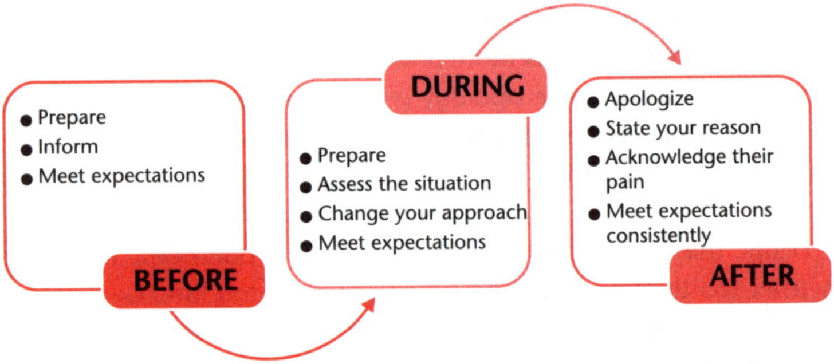

Fifthly, you need to now reflect the corrected image at each point of contact. Deliver on your promises consistently with each promise you make. Any deviation from this is enough to set you back and create a weak impression.

HAVING CONFLICTING TRIBES AND TRAITS

There are times when your only mistake is that you belong to a different tribe. But be assured the stranger may not be looking for that tribe or even may be too tired or stressed to pay enough attention and look beyond it.

Rethink the three factors of first impressions — the situation, you and the stranger. Determine what your image should have been. Rethink how the stranger had perceived your image. This analysis can help you correct this mistake in the future.

The first thing to do is to focus on the tribes that you share with the stranger. The second thing is to play down any tribe that could cause a poor first impression. This can be corrected through the elements whether it is clothing, grooming, body language, etiquette or vocal communication.

There are situations when the traits you would like to project might be in conflict with the stranger. For example, being respected and being liked are two different things. While it helps to be liked, you cannot ignore the importance of being respected.

A trait that is necessary in your business may be perceived a negative trait in your social life. For example, being a go-getter who seeks opportunities and makes the best use of them may be appreciated in your business life. It may not be ideal in your social life. Change your stance to meet the requirements of the situation.

We may, perhaps, commit a social faux pas without realizing it. On the whole, carrying a positive attitude and being courteous to others consistently gives people the chance to form positive impressions.

2. When to Ignore the Negative First Impression

Each of us wants to create powerful and positive first impressions. The assumption is that you and the stranger have the readiness and the capability to form a relationship. In the context of first impressions, it requires self-esteem and self-mastery at your end and an openness to accept you at the stranger's end.

But it is not possible to please everyone all the time. What comes in between could be the stranger and their prejudice; at other times it could be your low self-esteem and low self-mastery. In this case, both of you are moving away from each other and find it extremely difficult to create a healthy relationship. While the stranger is actually moving away from you, you will end up second guessing and making excessive efforts at building a relationship which has the unintentional effect of pushing the stranger further away from you.

Many times, low self-esteem affects how you read the stranger's perceptions. People with low levels of self-esteem may give greater importance to what other people think and say. They may perceive things which were never intended by the other person. They are likely to criticize themselves more frequently. Knowing when not to work towards changing a negative first impression comes with high levels of self-esteem and self-mastery which we talked about in Chapter 7 — Who I Am.

Readiness to Create a Relationship

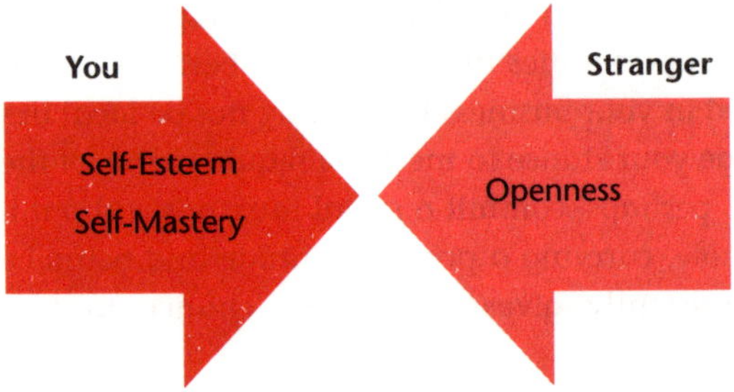

Speaking of prejudice, it denotes the intensity with which the stranger carries his stereotypes. Prejudice, by its very nature is unreasonable and is hard if not impossible to overcome. If we take a closer look at its meaning we discover that it means 'an adverse opinion or leaning formed without just grounds or before sufficient knowledge'. It also means 'an irrational attitude of hostility directed against an individual, a group, a race, or their supposed characteristics'[1].

Given that consistent efforts to change a negative first impression are based on rational influence, they fail to overturn prejudice. Prejudices are deeply held beliefs that create a sense of self for the stranger. As such, overcoming the prejudice requires the stranger to rethink his own sense of self. People resist such change. Hence, it requires a far larger effort than by a single individual and a far more momentous incident than small, consistent efforts to change a prejudice.

Don't be disheartened though. Make your effort. Continue with being consistent in projecting the image you need to project, but carry out your work with a positive attitude. If you continue with apologies and other efforts to meet the person midway, it is likely to be viewed as weakness and worsens the situation. As you continue with the work at hand or in your daily life, manage yourself and manage the situation.

You might ask, why should I be managing myself or the situation?

Truth about prejudice is that it can be extremely frustrating working or living with a person with a prejudice against you. It takes a great deal of self-esteem and self-mastery and the resultant patience to handle the person and keep the relationship going. Due to the poor impression the person forms out of prejudice, he is capable of making biased decisions which are not in your interest.

Don't let it affect your inner balance. Respond neutrally if you have to. If it is a work situation, make sure that other stakeholders such as your team mates, peers and bosses know your work and your neutral intention. This helps in the long run. If things are truly unmanageable, you may have to look for a different work opportunity. But, first try to manage the situation.

Rahul was a middle manager in the marketing department. With a new head of the marketing department joining the company, he looked forward to building a fresh relationship. Unfortunately, things took a wrong turn. The head seemed to feel that the current programmes were performing below par and ignoring the results, he went on to create a fresh marketing programme from scratch.

As the person who was handling the programmes in the temporary absence of a head, the implicit blame lay on Rahul although it seemed unfair. The more Rahul tried to make him understand the thought process behind the current programmes and the results, the worse the situation seemed to become.

Soon enough, the existing programmes were stopped midway and Rahul was seen in poor light. Apart from feeling that this was unhealthy for the company, Rahul felt personally slighted.

He thought about it over the weekend and realized that the marketing head was simply consolidating his position and showing his efforts by bringing his own version of the programmes. Rahul decided that there was little point in defending either himself or the old programme.

Inability to Create a Relationship

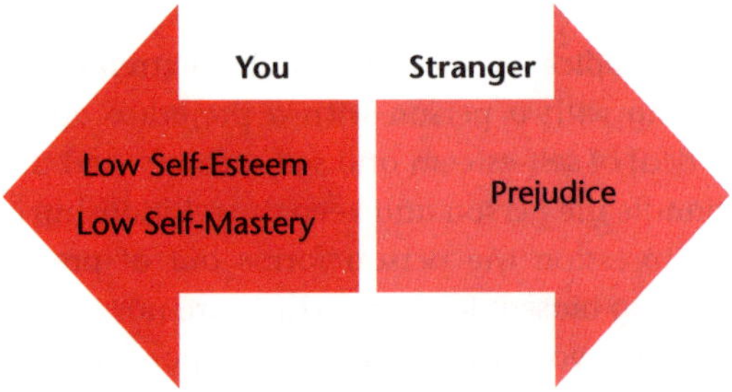

He decided to manage the situation as best he could and worked with the head to implement the new programme. Although the situation never became easy, it became more manageable between the two when the head realized that Rahul was working with him to implement the new programme.

While work situations give you the choice of leaving, in your personal lives leaving is probably the last choice. Prejudice in personal lives can cause extreme stress and pain. It is more important to maintain your self-esteem and self-mastery in these situations. Sometimes, the worst of situations relax after a period.

Whether it is business, social or personal lives, don't believe that you could approach a powerful or influential person to correct the situation. It would be at your risk. The answer is to keep things open for all to see, without talking behind the person. Make sure that communication is sent to all the relevant persons where possible. Senior executives don't need to know every incident. What they need is an awareness of the situation. This is enough for them to intervene when things come to a breaking point. It is for you to manage the situation and maintain the relationship.

Self-awareness becomes critical in these situations. In addition, handling the situation with self-mastery helps you manage the relationships well.

People ask us, "I am often told that I am overly sensitive, that I assume weak first impressions when that is not so. I end up apologizing where there is no cause for one. How do I avoid that?" Recognize that it is your low self-esteem which is the cause. Although unfortunate, this is all too frequent an occurrence. Within families, friends' circles and particularly in offices, it hurts relationships, by creating the impression that you are a weak individual in need of approval.

Sita carried a poor image of herself and she looked for opportunities to prove herself to her family and friends. Life was a constant state of worry about what her mother-in-law really meant with her comments. It could be as simple a comment as, "One does need to manage servants well to get good work out of them", when her mother-in-law was in conversation with the family.

Sita would assume that her mother-in-law was criticizing her. She would grow defensive and give justifications as to how she manages the servant. It affected her relationship with her mother-in-law. A defensive attitude that constantly tries to justify one's actions and words does not add up to warmth and commitment.

At the same time, for every comment that she made, Sita was in the constant habit of rehashing it after the visitor had left, worrying if the visitor took offense at what she had said. Over a phone call or on the next visit, she would bring up the old issue and give numerous apologies that put the visitor at great discomfort.

By trying too hard, she intruded into others' space. Her low self-esteem and the consequent worry interfered with the creation of healthy relationships. The image she projected was one of inability to read the other person's need and an obsession with her own words and actions. This was also the result of poor self-mastery.

Sita's case is an extreme but a very real example. You too might find yourself in situations of this kind when you are not at ease with yourself, or experience poor self-worth as you compare yourself to others.

Nothing harms an impression more than an apology where it is not needed. Observe yourself and recognize your discomfort. With self-mastery, you can ease the discomfort and even if it doesn't fully go away, you can certainly take the other's actions and words with the right perspective. Look at your self-esteem. Accept yourself for what you are.

Don't read too much between the lines. Many times what we think the person has assumed can be the opposite of what the person has perceived. Ignoring the cues sent out by the four elements and the inability to read the cues accurately can be the cause for this. Watch the stranger's actions and words and filter it as neutrally as possible to see their real perceptions. Pay attention to the cues. Depending on the situation, ask the person. Don't assume. At other times, ask a close friend who understands the situation for advice.

In the end, you cannot change the other person. So take the negative first impression in perspective, filter it through your feedback mechanism and make the necessary adjustments.

3. Creating Lasting Impressions

We would like to conclude by reiterating the importance of creating lasting good impressions whether through a positive first impression or by changing a negative first impression.

The common factor to both is to remain true to yourself. This is the most important rule of all. If you try to project an image that is contrary to your inner self, you will still reveal the real self through the cues given out by the four elements, your visual and verbal cues, sometimes even olfactory. Then the stranger will view you as insincere and hence, untrustworthy.

As well as you prepare to create great first impressions, you need to plan methodically for future impressions. While each future meeting may not have the same lasting impact as the first impression, add them all up and you can make them larger than their sum, helping you create a positive lasting impression. So, treat each future impression as a critical point and prepare well. If you let your guard down a single time, you are losing your future chances at creating a great lasting impression.

REFERENCE

1 http://www.merriam-webster.com/dictionary/prejudice

SO FAR

- Although first impressions are lasting impressions, with consistent effort, you can bring about a change in a negative first impression.
- Saying the wrong words, doing the wrong thing and belonging to conflicting tribes can lead to negative impressions.
- Carry a positive attitude, do not let temporary adversity affect your composure.
- Do not criticize or blame others.
- Do not attack others in heated discussions.
- Continue to project a positive image in all future interactions.
- Be careful when and what type of humour you use.
- Do not break promises. Meet your commitments.
- Live up to expectations. Show your capability through words and actions.
- Assess the stranger, the situation and yourself continuously and make the necessary changes.
- Apologies must be relevant and balanced. They must include the reason behind breaking a promise. Acknowledge how the person is affected. Move on with the task at hand. Deliver on future promises consistently.
- Positive impressions are difficult to create when you carry low self-esteem and self-mastery or when the stranger carries a prejudice.

Chapter 11

In Summary – Situations to Manage for Positive Lasting Impressions

Begin with the end in mind.

— Stephen Covey

We chose first impressions as the topic for our book because we had the end in mind. We recommend that you too keep the end, that is, your goals in mind. When your goals are clear, the road you need to take becomes clear as you move forward. In order to meet your goals of success, peace and meaning in life, first impressions play a key role.

When we work backwards, your goals determine the first impressions you need to create. These in turn determine the image you need to project. Projecting the right image requires the knowledge, understanding and implementation of the four elements of first impressions — clothing, grooming, body language including etiquette and vocal communication. The image you project influences your inner self. At the same time, you require self-esteem and self-mastery along with knowledge of yourself and the world to understand how to implement these four elements of first impressions.

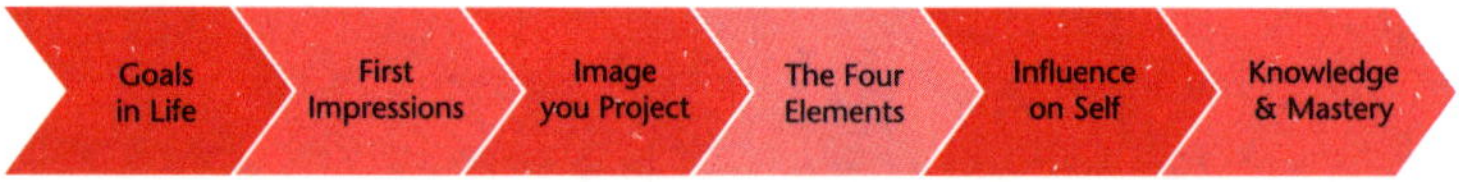

WORKING WITH THE END IN MIND

To summarize what we have talked about in the book, first impressions are impressions that strangers form of you within the first few seconds of meeting you. These impressions are based on the image you project. The four elements of first impressions — clothing, grooming, body language including etiquette as well as vocal communication help you project the right image.

To implement these elements effectively, you require knowledge and understanding of the *stranger,* the *situation* and *yourself.* Achieving this requires self-esteem and self-mastery.

The place you begin with is the inner *you,* in which you take a look at your strengths and weaknesses in general as well as those that are relevant to the particular situation you are about to face. You then take a look at the *situation and* know as much as you can about the *stranger* you are about to meet. Based on your goal for the situation, namely succeeding at the interview, making a sale, forming a relationship or simply creating a positive first impression at the party, you prepare for the occasion and project the appropriate image.

The image you project influences how you feel as well as your inner self, creating a self-fulfilling prophecy that works to your advantage. At the same time, the stranger, based on his experience, perceptions and his goal from the situation forms his first impression of you.

Our story began with these first impressions. In writing this book, we have taken an in-depth look at the goals that people choose to strive for in their lives. We arrived at the model for creating positive first impressions based on these goals and the situations that are relevant to attain them.

We have listed in this chapter, 21 situations that are common to many lives so that you have a quick guide at hand when you need it the most. We have grouped them into business, social, personal and public lives. These are situations where first impressions are critical for your success, happiness and peace of mind.

In discussing these situations, we address the key issues of the situation and hence the expectations of the stranger. This thought process has led to the questions below and our answers to them:

- What are the demands of the *situation*?
- What is the *stranger's* expectation for the given *situation*?
- What are *your* goals?
- Given these demands, expectations and goals, what should be *your* message?
- In order to communicate this message, how should *you* prepare and respond?

The situations, along with this practical detail, will help you perform a quick assessment of the situation you are about to face and prepare for it.

Business Lives

Our business lives are the source of our material success and form the largest part of our waking lives. As such, handling these lives well can lead us to productive and fruitful lives.

1. FACING INTERVIEWS

During interviews, companies look for competence, integrity and the cultural fit of the individual. Within the domain of competence, they could be looking for knowledge and experience within your function. You need to find out what competence means for the particular industry, company and the position you are appearing for. It could mean an aggressive adherence to timelines and targets in one company or position. In another company, it could mean diligence and near-perfection. The answers can also give you a clear picture of the company's culture. When it comes to integrity of the person, it is non-negotiable in all companies.

Each interviewer could be looking for a different aspect of you. For example, the human resources personnel could be assessing you for cultural fit while the departmental interview is more likely to focus on your competence. Based on these goals, the interviewers bring their experience, knowledge and perceptions to judge whether you are part of their tribe and whether they can meet their goals through you. In short, can they have a business relationship with you? Your goal is to gain the job offer.

Tip: Understand the industry, the company culture, the position and the persons interviewing you. Be prepared with the four elements of first impressions, but be prepared to shift gears and project the relevant tribe that you belong to, depending on the person interviewing you. Basic requirement is to show the interviewers that you belong to their tribe.

2. INTERVIEWING CANDIDATES

If you are conducting the interview, you would have experienced the fact that although millions of people struggle to find the right job, the task of getting the right candidate for your company is anything but simple. Interviews are as much about attracting the best talent as about choosing them.

The company and its employees need to project a powerful and positive image that attracts the best talent. As the interviewer, it is your job to project that image with the interviewees. Candidates look for rapidly growing companies, those which give them opportunities and a path for advancement, companies with an open atmosphere and little in terms of politics, a support system that helps them excel at their work and a good-to-work-for boss. Seems like a tall order. But, much of this is projected by the interviewer and how he or she handles the candidate.

Tip: Project the right image of authority with courtesy, straightforwardness and empathy to create positive and strong first impressions with each candidate whether he is the right fit or not. A negative impression does not take long to spread. Word-of-mouth is a strong force, wherein power is multiplied several times with the viral nature of Internet and social media.

3. MAKING A SALE

Sales is a critical function that requires the sales executive to be on the road practically all working days of the week, sometimes from early in the morning till late in the night. Despite this grueling schedule, successful sales executives prepare themselves for each meeting. They don't compromise on the clothing and grooming aspects either, in projecting the image of competence and dependability with potential clients. A poor image is the equivalent of applying brakes to a smoothly running car.

In addition to a strong product and dependable service, potential clients are looking for characteristics like knowledge, experience, competence, confidence, trustworthiness, diligence, and more, depending on the nature of the product, the industry they belong to and their business compulsions. They might be risk averse or may be willing to take a carefully calculated risk with a relatively unknown product or company for a lower price or better service. Their line of thought and decision-making impacts the image they seek.

Tip: Know the company goals and project the image that can give you a foothold in the company. Dress and act accordingly. When meeting a potential client, whether it is a person at the bottom of the purchase hierarchy or the head of purchasing himself, create positive first impressions with each. Even as the senior executive makes the final decision, he pays attention to his team's views since they perform the product and company assessment. Creating a weak to negative impression on them can lead to lost deals.

4. CUSTOMER IMPRESSIONS

It pays to retain current customers because it is less expensive selling to an existing customer than it is to attract a new customer. Current customers are the key to higher sales and profitability. Retaining these customers can be a comfortable or stressful task depending on their perceptions of your product, service and response. As the sales or customer service executive meeting these customers, remember that they value the traits of approachability, focus on their interests, product and service excellence, prompt response and trustworthy and straightforward nature.

Concern for first impressions is not limited to company employees. Professionals like doctors, lawyers, financial advisors and other consultants, benefit from projecting the appropriate image. Given this competitive world, all it takes is one poor response to create a negative impression and lose the customer. Hence, it is as important to reinforce positive impressions during each meeting as it is to creating positive first impressions.

Tip: If you are a company or an institution, ensure that a culture of customer service permeates the company. Make sure that each employee, both back-end and front-end executives, are trained in the art and science of image management.

If you are a customer-facing professional, while following the rules of the four elements of first impressions, treat your clients with courtesy, patience and promptness.

5. IMPRESSIONS WITH PEERS

The impressions you create with your peers are necessary stepping stones to your growth within the company. These are continuous impressions that you create with each project, meeting and interaction, leading to lasting impressions. Not only are they important in the rapport you build and hence the co-operation and support you receive, but also in projecting your competence in handling larger responsibilities. Projection of your competence, confidence and empathy takes you a long way in instilling confidence about your ability as well as building that much needed rapport.

Tip: Don't wait for formal meetings to meet colleagues from other departments. Drop in for a casual chat during lunch or tea time and get to know them well. These are times when information exchange takes place which never makes it to the formal channels of communication. It is the time to gain knowledge about their concerns and point of view. It also helps you bring them up-to-date with mutually relevant projects and seek their thoughts and support where necessary. Your body language and vocal communication comes in for special mention in building these informal networks within a company.

6. IMPRESSIONS WITH JUNIORS

The team reporting to you looks up to you for guidance and support. They also look at the respect you command from your peers and superiors. Thirdly, they look to you for consistency in how you deal with them. They want to know if you will stand by them and if you have their growth, pay hike and interests in mind.

Tip: You need to set an example for your team through the four elements of first impressions. Your body language and vocal communication become critical factors in how your team perceives you. You can be a hard task master, but coupled with empathy and guidance, you can create great, self-driven teams.

7. PROMOTIONS

While you work diligently at your current job, you are constantly being assessed for the next level in the hierarchy as are many others within the company or your team itself. Your seniors are looking not just for competence in the current job profile, but also whether you are ready for higher responsibilities. It could mean different things at different levels of the hierarchy. If you are a junior executive, they could be looking at your ability to handle a task independently. If you are a senior executive and the next promotion is to a managerial position, they could be looking for your ability to relate to your team and lead them effectively. At higher levels, the ability with which you deal with your colleagues, seniors, peers across industry, your strategic thinking could be under assessment.

Tip: Even as you work diligently at your current job, assess the requirements for the next level of hierarchy. Observe your seniors and learn from their knowledge and experience. Continuously build the capability and relationships needed and project the image of competence and readiness for the next level.

Always dress for the job you would like to reach at the next level, not just the current one you hold. Your superiors are looking for certainty that you can meet the demands of the new position, not just a promise. They do not want to lose a great executive for a poor manager. How you handle your current position only gives them a hint of what you can deliver, whereas dressing, walking and speaking at the higher level adds to the positive impression about your competence and readiness to take on higher responsibilities.

8. INDUSTRY EVENTS

Nowhere are first impressions more important than at conferences and exhibitions when you meet hundreds of strangers across a few days. They are the true test of your ability to project an image of credibility and create positive first impressions. You are a reflection of your company and people tend to remember the company positively, negatively or not at all based on the image you project. In the short-term, it is about positive word-of-mouth and in the long-term, it leads to higher sales and company recognition.

At exhibitions, it is about the number of people who stop at your stand and listen to your pitch. Jaded after having a look at hundreds of companies vying to talk to them, visitors are on the lookout for products that understand their story and solve their problems or deliver tangible benefits. This translates to empathy, straightforwardness and an ability to attract their attention in the midst of stiff competition.

In conferences, it is about the number of people who remember you after they leave the conference. Deep knowledge, experience, patience, courtesy, an interesting point of view and an ability to listen are some key factors that gain audience attention.

Tip: Approach people with a smile, talk to them and listen actively. Elicit their story with questions and draw them into conversations to help you understand them. This requires empathy, approachability and openness. Follow the dress code of your industry. It is generally formal wear in conferences and can be formal wear or company casuals, for example, T-shirts with company logo, depending on the industry, at exhibitions.

9. COLLEGE ADMISSIONS

College admissions are critical, make or break occasions. That you don't get a second chance to create a first impression is particularly true for college admissions whether for undergraduate or post graduate courses. The panel that assesses your group discussions, interviews and presentations looks for your knowledge, ability to think independently, diligence, maturity, respect for fellow students and teachers as well as empathy.

Tip: Although as teenagers, casual dressing seems to be the norm, it pays to be particularly attentive to the four elements of first impressions when it comes college admissions. These help you handle your group discussions, interviews and presentations if any, effectively. Be straightforward, honest, and courteous in your approach. It is better to admit that you don't know something than to try to bluff your way through. When it comes to group discussions, you need to be strong enough to convey your point of view, while giving a chance to other participants.

Social Lives

10. OFFICIAL DINNERS

Official dinners can be formal or semi-formal. The type of dinner event gives an indication of the people who would be present, their expectations from other guests and the etiquette. The key to successful social lives is adherence to etiquette and contributing positively to the conversations.

Formal dinners related to work could be in honour of a visiting senior official, to mark a significant event like the completion of certain years in existence, a large expansion and similar occasions. There is clear expectation of adherence to protocol since it is in respect to a person, organization and occasion. No rule of etiquette is more important than that of arriving on time for these events. Conversations that show your breadth and depth of not just knowledge, but also understanding of the issues are critical. You need to be interesting. At the same time, there is an expectation of respect to others' point of view and the courtesy of listening to them.

On the other hand, celebratory occasions like winning over a large client can be semi-formal. While rules of etiquette begin to relax here, you still need the art of effective conversations, particularly at semi-formal events. For informal events, it is expected that you enjoy the occasion within broad limits.

Tip: Know the protocol beforehand and prepare accordingly. Whatever the occasion, whether formal or semi-formal, it is the time to reach out to other guests. It is an opportunity for you to build contacts and form relationships with people in other fields. If it is your company or industry event, many of them will be your colleagues, superiors and peers. If it is a social event, you will have a chance to meet experts from other fields too, people you may not otherwise meet. These relationships are helpful for your long-term future.

11. INFORMAL EVENTS

Informal social events can range from events that mark an achievement to festivals celebrated as part of your business, social or personal lives to events that are meant simply to get to know one another in an informal atmosphere. It is a time to enjoy yourself and let others enjoy with you. Having a great time at a party is a necessary part of forming relationships that you are hard pressed to form in your daily life with its attendant responsibilities. That is the whole point of these occasions. Each of you would be involved in your daily responsibilities with little time for social interaction and to reveal your natural, relaxed side. These social occasions can lead to happy friendships and eventually deeper relationships with strangers, friends and family.

At these events, guests expect to have a good time. Being stiff and formal at these events will make you stand out like a sore thumb and cause discomfort to some guests. So, while you don't need to be the life of the party, you are definitely expected to lighten up and help others do so too. All this is expected to stay within limits so that no guest is put to discomfort.

Tip: Informal parties aren't only about having fun. There is a fairly informal code of dress, behaviour and etiquette. Adhering to it helps you fit in better, that is, belong to the tribe. Do too little and you will find little difference between your business and social lives. Be inappropriate in dress, behaviour or etiquette and you will find yourself in the wrong company with the strong possibility of not receiving another invite.

12. SPOUSE'S OFFICIAL PARTIES

These are an important part of life for any person with a working spouse. Don't for a moment think that it is the spouses' party and their affair. It becomes your responsibility too since most companies today, try to involve the family to a some extent. This brings about greater inclusion and not surprisingly, adds to the impressions your spouse creates with colleagues. From promotions to being included in the right circles and forming strong relationships, when you take an appropriately active role in your spouse's circle, it strengthens their success at work.

Depending on the company, you may be expected to circulate along with the spouse, mingle freely with the employees or stay with the other partners. By and large, these are not strict rules, but habits formed over time. It is fine not to stick to them rigidly, but observe the others before you deviate from the norm.

Tip: Prepare for your spouse's party as carefully as you would your own. Understand the nature of the event. Further, know who will be present, their background and interests and put them at ease. Make yourself a part of the event and form relationships with your spouse's colleagues and their spouses in turn. Be open and at ease. Also, be a good listener and a good conversationalist.

Personal Lives

13. DATING

Whatever decade of life you are in, dating is a time of apprehension mixed with excitement at the prospect of spending time with an interesting person. It can lead to a long-term friendship or a relationship and eventually marriage. Whether you are filled with excitement, apprehension, boredom or the negative feeling that it is a complete waste of time, your state of mind reflects in your behaviour and conversations with your date.

Dating comes with its own rules and expectations, depending on how well you know the person, how often you have been on a date with him or her and the expectations each of you brings to the date. Some begin as a clearly platonic relationship, while others are filled with excitement at the potential of a deep relationship. First time dates are a time when you skirt deeper issues and simply get to know each other from the surface. Future dates are a time to open up, depending on your comfort with the person. Stay too distant and shy, or get too close too soon and you can say good bye to any chance of a meaningful relationship.

Tip: Being at ease and being the interesting person that you are is very important to dating. Read the cues well. Does the person want to get closer, know more about you? Do they want to stick to the periphery? At the same time, what do you want to do? Are you comfortable with the person? Do you want to reveal more, such as the things that are important to you? Or do you want to continue things the way they are for now? The outcome of the date is decided based on these two factors — what your date wants and what you want.

You need not put everything in words. A date is the perfect example of an event where you let your non-verbal communication do the talking. Use the four elements of first impressions appropriately for the perfect date.

14. MEETING THE PROSPECTIVE SPOUSE

Whether you are meeting your future spouse in the presence of the families or by yourself, it can be an awkward moment. But nowhere are first impressions more important than on this occasion. It can be the beginning of a lifelong relationship and there are many expectations at this event. Meeting these expectations while retaining your personality can make for a healthy beginning to a strong relationship and this is made through positive first impressions.

Occasions that are part of tradition are usually steeped in long-standing customs. You would be ruffling quite a few feathers when you go against these customs. Ranging from how you dress, how you are groomed, your body language and etiquette to what you say and how you say it, there are unwritten rules for everything.

Tip: Know the rules by observing or asking others. You can make changes to them to reflect the real you, but it helps to retain those that matter to the families. You may want to do away with these rules and customs, but, if you want to bring the family together as a unit and blend into the unit, understanding and meeting the important parts of the customs is essential. Prepare in advance. Know the person and the family if the family is likely to be present. Be yourself and at ease without being casual. More importantly, listen to the person and the family with keen interest.

15. MEETING PROSPECTIVE IN-LAWS

Meeting your fiancé's family for the first time is an important occasion. Happy families aren't made of just the husband and wife, but involve maintaining healthy relationships with the entire family. These are made up of many positive first impressions, involving each member of the close family and consistent effort in sustaining these impressions.

Your future in-laws would want the best for their offspring, but you don't need to let that make you apprehensive. These occasions are generally not as formal as when the entire family is involved in making the event happen.

Tip: Know the expectations beforehand and dress appropriately. Taking gifts for the immediate family is a good idea. Be prepared and put your best foot forward. Most importantly, be at ease and put them at ease.

16. MARRIAGES

Marriages are a time of great expectation and promise. But, the event itself can range anywhere from a single day to several days of celebration. Much depends on how well the entire event is organized. There can be conflicting or too many expectations from either side. People might be hesitant to ask for clarifications from the other family and these turn into needless irritants.

Given all these factors, it can be a tiring and stressful time for the bride and the groom. They need to accommodate the expectations of family and in-laws which requires a great deal of patience. It is the first step into a lifelong relationship and taking the right steps go a long way in ensuring a promising future.

Tip: Whether you are the bride or the groom, you would naturally make sure that you are dressed and groomed to perfection. Make sure that you keep your family, in-laws and future spouse informed of all the major decisions. Many times, it is you and your future spouse who could be the conduit of information for each side. Manage with a smile and try not to wilt under the demands of either side.

17. NEW BEGINNINGS

If you have been divorced or widowed, there comes a time when you are ready to move on. You might be uncomfortable with the prospect of dating once again, putting your profile up on the marriage or dating sites or about having your family and friends play the role of match-makers. But, it is an essential part of moving on and it pays to prepare yourself mentally, emotionally and physically for this gradual process.

There are certain rules and guidelines to meeting people online. These could be about offering sufficient information about yourself without revealing the personal things until you know the person better, assessing the other person carefully and so on. Once you shortlist and decide to meet the person physically, the normal rules of dating apply. In matches arranged by the family, the expectation is that you will be ready to make a decision on your match based on very little data about them.

Tip: Letting go is the single largest healer in life. Once you are well along that road, it is time to be at ease with yourself, learn the art of dating and getting to know a person all over again. The four elements of first impressions are of great help in making this necessary new beginning in your life. Family and friends would be more than willing to help. It is good to take their help in this important part of your life.

18. FESTIVE OCCASIONS

Festive occasions are a time to celebrate with family, the extended family and friends. Whether you are attending a party or hosting one, it is a time to make sure everyone is comfortable and share the happy time with them. These occasions make for happy memories long after the event has passed and in strengthening your relationships.

Even though these occasions are related to your personal lives, rules and etiquette of social occasions apply here. If you are the guest, the expectations are that you arrive on time, offer help where necessary and mix with the rest of the family. If you are the host, depending on the occasion, you are expected to keep the arrangements tasteful, on time and in the required quantity, welcome the guests, make sure they are comfortable and that the event goes off without a hitch.

Tip: Take care of your dress and grooming, spend time with each person at the occasion, help the host if you are a guest, take help from your guests if you are hosting the occasion and make sure that everyone has a good time.

19. MANAGING TEENS & YOUNG ADULTS

You need to manage your children, their dressing and etiquette, more than you manage yours. This is true from their childhood to late adolesence. Teens and young adults start to exercise their independence and clothing is normally the first target for them. To your consternation, they are happy to be dressed in torn jeans, clunky jewellery and accessories that don't seem worth half the price they paid for it. They are probably too casual and you worry whether they will pay attention to the guests or sit in a corner glued to their cell phone; whether they will treat elders respectfully or are at their casual best. You are right to think that such behaviour needs correction in their best interest.

But, they too have their tribes and it is critical for them to fit into their tribes. There isn't much you can do about that, nor is it advisable to lay down rigid rules. It only stifles them and leads to rebellion, quiet or visible. But, it is important to set boundaries and instill your value system.

Tip: First, understand them and the boundaries they set for themselves. You would be surprised to learn that for all their casual behaviour and rejection of authority, they do have a set of values and boundaries for themselves. Where you feel these boundaries fall short, continue to communicate the right values to them at the right moments.

Practice some give and take. Allow them to make their decisions so long as the decisions are harmless. Ask them to follow guidelines in other aspects, say attending family occasions in the proper attire, being polite and considerate, spending time with elders, lending a helping hand and so on. So long as they feel you understand them and that you are not out to stifle them, they will generally meet you almost halfway and that's a lot to expect.

Public Lives

20. SPEAKING AT CONFERENCES

If you are a speaker, moderator or panel member at a conference, the audience is not one or two, but potentially hundreds. You would be well-prepared with your speech based on your knowledge of the subject and the audience. But depending on whether you are able to involve the audience in your topic, you could end up just another speaker or one who is remembered long after the event concludes.

The nature of the topic, your position in the line of speakers and the type of audience, each is a factor that determines your success as a speaker.

Tip: Public speeches are a matter of involving the audience and carrying them with your story or line of thought. From reaching out to the audience before, during and after your time on stage, to your dress, grooming, body language including etiquette and vocal communication, you can make a real and lasting impact with the audience.

21. MEETING THE MEDIA

Whether you are on air, on social media or speaking to the print media, the single most important difference between these and other occasions is your inability to see the audience. You cannot see them or hear them until after you speak and hence cannot make adjustments to what you say or how you say it. Yet, your word can have wide readership and viewership and carry positive or negative impact. Your words will remain as evidence in seeming perpetuity as they are posted, shared, commented upon, discussed and tweeted.

A lot depends on the context of what you say and how you say it. It is also about how the media perceives you and your words and the meaning they give to your words.

Tip: Understanding the audience, the media and the context is an essential requirement in these occasions. Being positive, open and straightforward in your comments goes a long way in bringing out the positive and deeper aspects of what you have to say. Meaning is also derived from how you are dressed and groomed. Make these elements work to your advantage.

The four elements of first impressions — clothing, grooming, body language including etiquette as well as vocal communication play an important role in preparing for these crucial occasions. They help you project the appropriate image at each occasion and with each stranger. This in turn helps you create positive first impressions and sustain them with positive lasting impressions.

It is important to remember that you are responsible for the image you project and hence the first impressions that are created. Make a conscious effort so that you are in control of what others see. Don't leave it to random chance. Your diligent effort pays off in the form of success in meeting your goals in life.

Making the Most of the List

While the above situations can be a quick reference, the most effective way to learn and correct yourself is by planning ahead, preparing, acting and once the event is over, to learn from what worked and what didn't.

We suggest that you maintain a diary in which you make a habit of noting the key situations you are about to face during the day, your goals for these situations and your preparation for each. At the end of the day, note down the results and your perception of how the situation went, what worked and what didn't and the required corrections. This approach helps you enhance your success with first impressions with great speed. We have filled a representative chart for clarity.

Situation	Objective	People	Message	Effort
Interview for the position of Marketing Manager	Job offer at a salary of ₹6 lakh	Head — Sales & Marketing, HR Head	• Efficient • Culture is of an aggressive sales force that drives marketing • Independent in decision-making and execution • Creative in finding solutions • Effective communication within team and across teams • Up-to-date with latest methods and metrics	• Dress softly tailored as sales people do, since the primary customer for the marketing person is the sales force • Black or navy blue trouser, cream shirt. Keep spare shirt at office since interview is in the evening
Informal weekend music evening at a friend's place	Enjoying the music with the guests	Host, guests	• Bring your music along to share with others • A blend of the formal and casual to reflect in clothing	• Dress in social casual clothes. • Dark jeans, white V-neck T-shirt, black jacket, black slip-ons in leather.

These are a few representative occasions and events you face in your lives. Depending on the individual differences in your business, social, personal and public lives, you face many versions of these events.

Conclusion

We constantly project an image of ourselves whether we aim to project one or not. People are forming their first and lasting impressions of us based on this image, impacting the kind of relationships we form and the success we attain.

It is in our hands to consciously project the appropriate image to create positive first impressions that help us achieve our goals and form deep and satisfying relationships.